STECK-VAUGHN

TABE®
Fundamentals

Focus on Skills

Math Computation

LEVEL M

2nd Edition

STECK-VAUGHN

TABE®
Fundamentals

Focus on Skills

Math Computation

LEVEL M

2nd Edition

Steck Vaughn™

HOUGHTON MIFFLIN HARCOURT
Supplemental Publishers

www.SteckVaughn.com
800-531-5015

Reviewers

Victor Gathers
> Regional Coordinator of Adult Services
> New York City Department of Education
> Brooklyn Adult Learning Center
> Brooklyn, New York

Brannon Lentz
> Assistant Director of Adult Education/Skills Training
> Northwest Shoals Community College
> Muscle Shoals, Alabama

Jean Pierre-Pipkin, Ed.D.
> Director of Beaumont I.S.D. Adult Education
> Cooperative Consortium
> Beaumont, Texas

ISBN-13: 978-1-4190-5355-9
ISBN-10:   1-4190-5355-8

Contents

To the Learner

Congratulations on your decision to study for the TABE! You are taking an important step in your educational career. This book will help you do your best on the TABE. You'll also find hints and strategies that will help you prepare for test day. Practice these skills—your success lies in your hands.

What Is the TABE?

TABE stands for the Tests of Adult Basic Education. These paper-and-pencil tests, published by McGraw-Hill, measure your progress on basic skills. There are five tests in all: Reading, Mathematics Computation, Applied Mathematics, Language, and Spelling.

TABE Levels M, D, and A

Test	Number of Items	Suggested Working Time (in minutes)
1 Reading	50	50
2 Mathematics Computation	25	15
3 Applied Mathematics	50	50
4 Language	55	39
5 Spelling	20	10

Test 1 Reading

This test measures basic reading skills. The main concepts covered by this test are word meaning, critical thinking, and understanding basic information.

Many things on this test will look familiar to you. They include documents and forms necessary to your everyday life, such as directions, bank statements, maps, and consumer labels. The test also includes items that measure your ability to find and use information from a dictionary, table of contents, or library computer display. The TABE also tests a learner's understanding of fiction and nonfiction passages.

Test 2 Mathematics Computation

Test 2 covers adding, subtracting, multiplying, and dividing. On the test you must use these skills with whole numbers, fractions, decimals, integers, and percents.

The skills covered in the Mathematics Computation test are the same skills you use daily to balance your checkbook, double a recipe, or fix your car.

Test 3 Applied Mathematics

The Applied Mathematics test links mathematical ideas to real-world situations. Many things you do every day require basic math. Making budgets, cooking, and doing your taxes all take math. The test also covers pre-algebra, algebra, and geometry. Adults need to use all these skills.

Some questions will relate to one theme. For example, auto repairs could be the subject and the question could focus on the repair schedule. You may be told when a car was last repaired and how often it needs to be repaired. You might have to predict the next maintenance date.

Many of the items will not require you to use a specific strategy or formula to get the correct answer. Instead this test challenges you to use your own problem-solving strategies to answer the question.

Test 4 Language

The Language test asks you to analyze different types of writing. Examples are business letters, resumes, job reports, and essays. For each task, you have to show you understand good writing skills.

The questions fit adult interests and concerns. Some questions ask you to think about what is wrong in the written material. In other cases, you will correct sentences and paragraphs.

Test 5 Spelling

In everyday life, you need to spell correctly, especially in the workplace. The spelling words on this test are words that many people misspell and words that are commonly used in adult writing.

Test-Taking Tips

1. Read the directions very carefully. Make sure you read through them word for word. If you are not sure what the question says, ask the person giving the test to explain it to you.

2. Read each question carefully. Make sure you know what it means and what you have to do.

3. Read all of the answers carefully, even if you think you know the answer.

4. Make sure that the reading supports your answer. Don't answer without checking the reading. Don't rely only on outside knowledge.

5. Answer all of the questions. If you can't find the right answer, rule out the answers that you know are wrong. Then try to figure out the right answer. If you still don't know, make your best guess.

6. If you can't figure out the answer, put a light mark by the question and come back to it later. Erase your marks before you finish.

7. Don't change an answer unless you are sure your first answer is wrong. Usually your first idea is the correct answer.

8. If you get nervous, stop for a while. Take a few breaths and relax. Then start working again.

How to Use *TABE Fundamentals*

Step-by-Step Instruction In Levels M and D, each lesson starts with step-by-step instruction on a skill. The instruction contains examples and then a test example with feedback. This instruction is followed by practice questions. Work all of the questions in the lesson's practice and then check your work in the Answers and Explanations in the back of the book.

The Level A books contain practice for each skill covered on the TABE. Work all of the practice questions and then check your work in the Answers and Explanations in the back of the book.

Reviews The lessons in Levels M and D are grouped by a TABE Objective. At the end of each TABE Objective, there is a Review. Use these Reviews to find out if you need to review any of the lessons before continuing.

Performance Assessment At the end of every book, there is a special section called the Performance Assessment. This section is similar to the TABE test. It has the same number and type of questions. This assessment will give you an idea of what the real test is like.

Answer Sheet At the back of the book is a practice bubble-in answer sheet. Practice bubbling in your answers. Fill in the answer sheet carefully. For each answer, mark only one numbered space on the answer sheet. Mark the space beside the number that corresponds to the question. Mark only one answer per question. On the real TABE, if you have more than one answer per question, they will be scored as incorrect. Be sure to erase any stray marks.

Strategies and Hints Pay careful attention to the TABE Strategies and Hints throughout this book. Strategies are test-taking tips that help you do better on the test. Hints give you extra information about a skill.

Setting Goals

On the following page is a form to help you set your goals. Setting goals will help you get more from your work in this book.

Section 1. Why do you want to do well on the TABE? Take some time now to set your short-term and long-term goals on page 3.

Section 2. Making a schedule is one way to set priorities. Deadlines will help you stay focused on the steps you need to take to reach your goals.

Section 3. Your goals may change over time. This is natural. After a month, for example, check the progress you've made. Do you need to add new goals or make any changes to the ones you have? Checking your progress on a regular basis helps you reach your goals.

For more information on setting goals, see Steck-Vaughn's *Start Smart Goal Setting Strategies*.

1. Set Your Goals

What is your long-term goal for using this book?

_____
_____
_____
_____

Complete these areas to identify the smaller steps to take to reach your long-term goal.

Content area	What I Know	What I Want to Learn
Reading	_____	_____
Language	_____	_____
Spelling	_____	_____
Math	_____	_____
Other	_____	_____

2. Make a Schedule

Set some deadlines for yourself.

For a 20-week planning calendar, see Steck-Vaughn's *Start Smart Planner*.

Goals	Begin Date	End Date
_____	_____	_____
_____	_____	_____
_____	_____	_____
_____	_____	_____

3. Celebrate Your Success

Note the progress you've made. If you made changes in your goals, record them here.

_____
_____
_____
_____

To the Instructor

About TABE

The Tests of Adult Basic Education are designed to meet the needs of adult learners in ABE programs. Written and designed to be relevant to adult learners' lives and interests, this material focuses on the life, job, academic, and problem-solving skills that the typical adult needs.

Because of the increasing importance of thinking skills in any curriculum, *TABE Fundamentals* focuses on critical thinking throughout each TABE Objective.

The TABE identifies the following thinking processes as essential to learning and achieving goals in daily life:

- ✦ Gather Information
- ✦ Organize Information
- ✦ Analyze Information
- ✦ Generate Ideas
- ✦ Synthesize Elements
- ✦ Evaluate Outcomes

Test 1 Reading

The TABE measures an adult's ability to understand home, workplace, and academic texts. The ability to construct meaning from prose and visual information is also covered through reading and analyzing diagrams, maps, charts, forms, and consumer materials.

Test 2 Mathematics Computation

This test covers whole numbers, decimals, fractions, integers, percents, and algebraic expressions. Skills are carefully targeted to the appropriate level of difficulty.

Test 3 Applied Mathematics

This test emphasizes problem-solving and critical-thinking skills, with a focus on the life-skill applications of mathematics. Estimation and pattern-recognition skills also are important on this test.

Test 4 Language

The Language test focuses on writing and effective communication. Students examine writing samples that need revision, with complete-sentence and paragraph contexts for the various items. The test emphasizes editing, proofreading, and other key skills. The context of the questions are real-life settings appropriate to adults.

Test 5 Spelling

This test focuses on the words learners most typically misspell. In this way, the test identifies the spelling skills learners most need in order to communicate effectively. Items typically present high-frequency words in short sentences.

Uses of the TABE

There are three basic uses of the TABE:

Instructional

From an instructional point of view, the TABE allows instructors to assess students' entry levels as they begin an adult program. The TABE also allows instructors to diagnose learners' strengths and weaknesses in order to determine appropriate areas to focus instruction. Finally the TABE allows instructors and institutions to monitor learners' progress.

Administrative

The TABE allows institutions to assess classes in general and measure the effectiveness of instruction and whether learners are making progress.

Governmental

The TABE provides a means of assessing a school's or program's effectiveness.

The National Reporting System (NRS) and the TABE

Adult education and literacy programs are federally funded and thus accountable to the federal government. The National Reporting System monitors adult education. Developed with the help of adult educators, the NRS sets the reporting requirements for adult education programs around the country. The information collected by the NRS is used to assess the effectiveness of adult education programs and make necessary improvements.

A key measure defined by the NRS is educational gain, which is an assessment of the improvement in learners' reading, writing, speaking, listening, and other skills during their instruction. Programs assess educational gain at every stage of instruction.

NRS Functioning Level	Grade Level	TABE (7/8 and 9/10) scale scores
Beginning ABE Literacy	0–1.9	Reading . . . . 367 and below Total Math . . . . 313 and below Language . . . . . 392 and below
Beginning Basic Education	2–3.9	Reading . . . . 368–460 Total Math . . . . 314–441 Language 393–490
Low Intermediate Basic Education	4–5.9	Reading . . . . 461–517 Total Math . . . . 442–505 Language 491–523
High Intermediate Basic Education	6–8.9	Reading . . . . 518–566 Total Math . . . . 506–565 Language 524–559
Low Adult Secondary Education	9–10.9	Reading . . . . 567–595 Total Math . . . . 566–594 Language 560–585

According to the NRS guidelines, states select the method of assessment appropriate for their needs. States can assess educational gain either through standardized tests or through performance-based assessment. Among the standardized tests typically used under NRS guidelines is the TABE, which meets the NRS standards both for administrative procedures and for scoring.

The three main methods used by the NRS to collect data are the following:

1. **Direct program reporting,** from the moment of student enrollment
2. **Local follow-up surveys,** involving learners' employment or academic goals
3. **Data matching,** or sharing data among agencies serving the same clients so that outcomes unique to each program can be identified.

Two of the major goals of the NRS are academic achievement and workplace readiness. Educational gain is a means to reaching these goals. As learners progress through the adult education curriculum, the progress they make should help them either obtain or keep employment or obtain a diploma, whether at the secondary school level or higher. The TABE is flexible enough to meet both the academic and workplace goals set forth by the NRS.

Using *TABE Fundamentals*

Adult Basic Education Placement
From the outset, the TABE allows effective placement of learners. You can use the *TABE Fundamentals* series to support instruction of those skills where help is needed.

High School Equivalency
Placement often involves predicting learners' success on the GED, the high school equivalency exam. Each level of *TABE Fundamentals* covers Reading, Language, Spelling, Applied and Computational Math to allow learners to focus their attention where it is needed.

Assessing Progress
Each TABE skill is covered in a lesson. These lessons are grouped by TABE Objective. At the end of each TABE Objective, there is a Review. Use these Reviews to find out if the learners need to review any of the skills before continuing.

At the end of the book, there is a special section called the Performance Assessment. This section is similar to the TABE test. It has the same number and type of questions. You can use the Performance Assessment as a timed pretest or posttest with your learners, or as a more general review for the actual TABE.

Steck-Vaughn's *TABE Fundamentals* Program at a Glance

The charts on the following page provide a quick overview of the elements of Steck-Vaughn's *TABE Fundamentals* series. Use this chart to match the TABE objectives with the skill areas for each level. This chart will come in handy whenever you need to find which objectives fit the specific skill areas you need to cover.

Steck-Vaughn's *TABE Fundamentals* Program at a Glance

TABE OBJECTIVE	Level M		Level D		Level A
	Reading	Language and Spelling	Reading	Language and Spelling	Reading, Language, and Spelling
Reading					
Interpret Graphic Information	✦		✦		✦
Words in Context	✦		✦		✦
Recall Information	✦		✦		✦
Construct Meaning	✦		✦		✦
Evaluate/Extend Meaning	✦		✦		✦
Language					
Usage		✦		✦	✦
Sentence Formation		✦		✦	✦
Paragraph Development		✦		✦	✦
Punctuation and Capitalization		✦		✦	✦
Writing Convention		✦		✦	
Spelling					
Vowel		✦		✦	✦
Consonant		✦		✦	✦
Structural Unit		✦		✦	✦

TABE OBJECTIVE	Level M		Level D		Level A
	Math Computation	Applied Math	Math Computation	Applied Math	Computational and Applied Math
Mathematics Computation					
Addition of Whole Numbers	✦				
Subtraction of Whole Numbers	✦				
Multiplication of Whole Numbers	✦		✦		
Division of Whole Numbers	✦		✦		
Decimals	✦		✦		✦
Fractions	✦		✦		✦
Integers			✦		✦
Percents			✦		✦
Orders of Operation			✦		✦
Applied Mathematics					
Number and Number Operations		✦		✦	✦
Computation in Context		✦		✦	✦
Estimation		✦		✦	✦
Measurement		✦		✦	✦
Geometry and Spatial Sense		✦		✦	✦
Data Analysis		✦		✦	✦
Statistics and Probability		✦		✦	✦
Patterns, Functions, Algebra		✦		✦	✦
Problem Solving and Reasoning		✦		✦	✦

Lesson 1 Addition of Whole Numbers—No Regrouping

It's Friday night at the Monroe High School football game, and you're in charge of finding out how many people came through both gates. At the south gate, 742 fans entered, and 214 fans entered the north gate. How many fans in all came through both gates?

On the TABE, you will be asked to add two or more numbers. The numbers may be arranged in a row or a column.

Row Addition
742 + 214 =

Column Addition
742
+ 214

Example Add. 742 + 214 =

1. Line up the digits. Add the ones. 2 + 4 = 6

```
hundreds tens ones
    7    4    2
  + 2    1    4
              6
```

2. Add the tens. 4 + 1 = 5

```
hundreds tens ones
    7    4    2
  + 2    1    4
         5    6
```

3. Add the hundreds. 7 + 2 = 9

```
hundreds tens ones
    7    4    2
  + 2    1    4
    9    5    6
```

742 + 214 = 956 fans who came through both gates.

Test Example

Add. Circle the answer.

1
20 + 4,002 + 210 + 17 =

A 9,802

B 6,472

C 4,294

D 4,249

E None of these

TABE Strategy

Read all the options carefully before choosing one. Options often look alike. For example, options C and D in question 1 are easy to confuse.

```
1  D        20
        4,002
          210
      +    17
        4,249
```

Practice

Add. Circle the answer.

1

$$6,113 \atop + 3,476$$

- A 3,363
- B 9,369
- C 3,633
- D 9,589
- E None of these

2

$924 + 63 =$

- F 1,550
- G 978
- H 1,554
- J 941
- K None of these

3

$41 + 103 + 2,100 + 304 =$

- A 2,347
- B 9,270
- C 5,580
- D 2,404
- E None of these

4

$$2,941 \atop + 6,058$$

- F 9,999
- G 8,997
- H 4,917
- J 8,999
- K None of these

5

$102 + 510 + 27 + 1,020 =$

- A 1,659
- B 9,840
- C 1,557
- D 7,167
- E None of these

6

$637 + 21 =$

- F 427
- G 616
- H 847
- J 658
- K None of these

7

$734 + 32 =$

- A 702
- B 766
- C 1,054
- D 414
- E None of these

8

$$5,871 \atop + 4,103$$

- F 1,772
- G 9,973
- H 9,772
- J 5,974
- K None of these

9

$360 + 3,006 + 11 + 202 =$

- A 3,573
- B 9,726
- C 3,579
- D 6,279
- E None of these

10

$$1,352 \atop + 7,506$$

- F 8,858
- G 5,884
- H 6,254
- J 8,588
- K None of these

Check your answers on page 49.

Lesson 2 Addition of Whole Numbers—Regrouping

Often when you add numbers, their sum is 10 or greater. For example, 9 ones plus 5 ones equals 14 ones. You can't write 14 in the ones column because only one digit will fit. However, 14 ones is the same as 1 ten and 4 ones. So you can regroup by adding 1 ten, or unit, to the tens column and 4 ones to the ones column. Some questions on the TABE will require you to regroup.

Example Add. 619 + 182 =

1. Line up the digits. Add the ones. 9 + 2 = 11. Write 1 below the ones column. Regroup 1 to the tens column.

```
    hundreds tens ones
              1
        6    1    9
      + 1    8    2
                  1
```

2. Add the tens. 1 + 1 + 8 = 10. Write 0 below the tens column. Regroup 1 to the hundreds column.

```
    hundreds tens ones
        1    1
        6    1    9
      + 1    8    2
             0    1
```

3. Add the hundreds. 1 + 6 + 1 = 8

```
    hundreds tens ones
        1    1
        6    1    9
      + 1    8    2
        8    0    1
```

619 + 182 = 801

Test Example

Add. Circle the answer.

1
```
        9
   + 3,842
```

A 3,951
B 3,841
C 3,941
D 3,851
E None of these

TABE Strategy

If your answer doesn't match any of the answer choices, check your work before you choose *None of these.*

1 D
```
            1
           9
    + 3,842
      3,851
```

Practice

Add. Circle the answer.

1

$582 + 245 =$

- A 847
- B 745
- C 727
- D 928
- E None of these

2

$7,528 + 7 =$

- F 7,625
- G 7,535
- H 7,526
- J 7,536
- K None of these

3

$7 + 6 + 3 =$

- A 13
- B 17
- C 16
- D 23
- E None of these

4

$$\begin{array}{r} 7 \\ + 9,628 \end{array}$$

- F 9,635
- G 9,625
- H 9,626
- J 9,726
- K None of these

5

$5 + 9 + 6 =$

- A 14
- B 21
- C 20
- D 15
- E None of these

6

$$\begin{array}{r} 9 \\ + 4,887 \end{array}$$

- F 5,886
- G 4,897
- H 4,986
- J 4,997
- K None of these

7

$738 + 143 =$

- A 982
- B 971
- C 871
- D 881
- E None of these

8

$892 + 9 =$

- F 901
- G 891
- H 991
- J 902
- K None of these

9

$$\begin{array}{r} 6 \\ + 5,256 \end{array}$$

- A 5,366
- B 5,252
- C 5,266
- D 5,262
- E None of these

10

$863 + 9 =$

- F 962
- G 972
- H 862
- J 873
- K None of these

Check your answers on page 49.

Add. Circle the answer.

1   5,876 + 6 =
    A 5,872
    B 5,972
    C 5,982
    D 5,876
    E None of these

2   654 + 43 =
    F 1,074
    G 697
    H 224
    J 1,084
    K None of these

3
$$\begin{array}{r} 8 \\ + 6{,}584 \\ \hline \end{array}$$
    A 6,682
    B 6,592
    C 6,584
    D 6,594
    E None of these

4   5,001 + 12 + 250 + 104 =
    F 5,367
    G 8,553
    H 9,741
    J 5,166
    K None of these

5   684 + 9 =
    A 783
    B 694
    C 693
    D 793
    E None of these

6   9,423 + 7 =
    F 9,431
    G 9,429
    H 9,420
    J 9,430
    K None of these

7
$$\begin{array}{r} 295 \\ + 433 \\ \hline \end{array}$$
    A 637
    B 628
    C 728
    D 639
    E None of these

8   4,952 + 9 =
    F 4,952
    G 4,960
    H 4,951
    J 4,961
    K None of these

9   356 + 527 =
    A 873
    B 882
    C 782
    D 973
    E None of these

10

$451 + 34 =$

F 781
G 475
H 485
J 791
K None of these

11

$444 + 657 =$

A 1,111
B 1,102
C 1,100
D 1,011
E None of these

12

$106 + 50 + 230 + 1,602 =$

F 9,962
G 1,988
H 9,902
J 3,958
K None of these

13

$5 + 8 + 4 =$

A 13
B 17
C 18
D 20
E None of these

14

$$\begin{array}{r} 4,472 \\ + 1,223 \\ \hline \end{array}$$

F 5,665
G 3,251
H 5,695
J 3,691
K None of these

15

$297 + 333 =$

A 620
B 621
C 603
D 602
E None of these

16

$596 + 7 =$

F 604
G 603
H 593
J 693
K None of these

17

$8 + 7 + 6 =$

A 21
B 23
C 13
D 15
E None of these

18

$$\begin{array}{r} 6,213 \\ + 1,756 \\ \hline \end{array}$$

F 7,868
G 7,969
H 7,696
J 7,879
K None of these

Check your answers on pages 49–50.

TABE Review: Addition of Whole Numbers •

Lesson 3 Subtraction of Whole Numbers—No Regrouping

How do you find the difference between how much money you earn every week and how much you have left after taxes? You use subtraction to find the difference.

Row Subtraction   Column Subtraction
$86 - 65 =$ 86
$\underline{-\ 65}$

Example Subtract. $86 - 65 =$

1. Line up the digits. Subtract the ones. $6 - 5 = 1$. Write 1 below the line in the ones place.

tens ones
8   6
$\underline{-\ 6 \qquad 5}$
1

2. Subtract the tens. $8 - 6 = 2$. Write 2 below the line in the tens place.

tens ones
8   6
$\underline{-\ 6 \qquad 5}$
2   1

$86 - 65 = 21$

Test Example

Subtract. Circle the answer.

1.
184
$\underline{-\ \ 72}$

A 111
B 112
C 116
D 122
E None of these

TABE Strategy

Check the answers to subtraction problems by adding. Example: Subtract $99 - 66 = 33$. To check, add $33 + 66 = 99$.

1 B   184
$\underline{-\ \ 72}$
112

Subtract. Circle the answer.

1

$$93 - 72$$

A 25
B 31
C 35
D 21
E None of these

2

$$5,671 - 40 =$$

F 5,271
G 5,631
H 1,671
J 5,641
K None of these

3

$$56 - 22$$

A 34
B 44
C 35
D 23
E None of these

4

$$7,625 - 2,404 =$$

F 5,222
G 5,221
H 5,329
J 5,201
K None of these

5

$$957 - 231$$

A 726
B 626
C 788
D 636
E None of these

6

$$9,380 - 20 =$$

F 7,380
G 9,360
H 9,180
J 7,180
K None of these

7

$$4,937 - 2,413 =$$

A 2,425
B 2,523
C 2,444
D 6,524
E None of these

8

$$491 - 180$$

F 310
G 571
H 311
J 511
K None of these

9

$$86 - 41$$

A 55
B 54
C 45
D 35
E None of these

10

$$761 - 521$$

F 241
G 282
H 230
J 240
K None of these

Check your answers on page 50.

Subtraction of Whole Numbers—Regrouping

Sometimes in subtraction, the number you are subtracting in a column is greater than the number from which you are subtracting. In such cases, you have to regroup before you can subtract. When you regroup, you borrow 10 ones from the next highest place value and add it to the next lower place value. Now you can subtract.

Example Subtract. 846 − 753 =

1. Line up the digits. Subtract the ones.
6 − 3 = 3

```
hundreds  tens  ones
    8       4      6
 −  7       5      3
                   3
```

2. To subtract the tens, borrow 1 from the hundreds. Now there are 14 tens.
14 − 5 = 9 tens.

```
          7    14
hundreds  tens  ones
    8       4      6
 −  7       5      3
            9      3
```

3. Subtract the hundreds. 7 − 7 = 0. You don't write a 0 in front of whole numbers, so leave the hundreds column blank.

```
          7    14
hundreds  tens  ones
    8       4      6
 −  7       5      3
            9      3
```

846 − 753 = 93

Test Example

Subtract. Circle the answer.

1

```
  432
−  19
```

A 423

B 427

C 413

D 412

E None of these

```
            2 12
1   C    432
        −  19
           413
```

Subtract. Circle the answer.

1

$$\begin{array}{r} 781 \\ -\ 29 \end{array}$$

A 752
B 810
C 768
D 762
E None of these

2

$$\begin{array}{r} 145 \\ -\ 97 \end{array}$$

F 242
G 37
H 48
J 152
K None of these

3

$7,649 - 477 =$

A 7,172
B 7,272
C 7,162
D 7,282
E None of these

4

$2,584 - 399 =$

F 2,285
G 1,285
H 2,215
J 2,185
K None of these

5

$$\begin{array}{r} 335 \\ -\ 41 \end{array}$$

A 376
B 314
C 294
D 394
E None of these

6

$5,259 - 867 =$

F 5,612
G 4,382
H 4,329
J 5,192
K None of these

7

$$\begin{array}{r} 131 \\ -\ 48 \end{array}$$

A 82
B 83
C 179
D 93
E None of these

8

$$\begin{array}{r} 849 \\ -\ 62 \end{array}$$

F 787
G 911
H 887
J 778
K None of these

9

$8,271 - 643 =$

A 7,628
B 8,638
C 8,628
D 7,638
E None of these

10

$6,518 - 471 =$

F 6,047
G 6,437
H 6,989
J 6,147
K None of these

Check your answers on page 50.

Subtract. Circle the answer.

1

357
− 29

A 338
B 332
C 386
D 327
E None of these

2

67
− 54

F 24
G 13
H 3
J 17
K None of these

3

518
− 97

A 615
B 411
C 531
D 421
E None of these

4

4,919 − 16 =

F 4,903
G 3,319
H 4,923
J 4,859
K None of these

5

1,641 − 568 =

A 1,063
B 1,172
C 1,572
D 1,163
E None of these

6

853
− 150

F 703
G 903
H 953
J 753
K None of these

7

2,961 − 1,710 =

A 2,271
B 1,250
C 3,250
D 1,251
E None of these

8

627
− 56

F 683
G 671
H 581
J 631
K None of these

9

6,558 − 24 =

A 6,535
B 4,158
C 6,418
D 6,544
E None of these

10

$8,249 - 7,206 =$

F 1,403
G 1,204
H 1,043
J 1,243
K None of these

11

589
− 244

A 355
B 345
C 344
D 354
E None of these

12

$9,461 - 520 =$

F 9,141
G 9,941
H 9,981
J 8,941
K None of these

13

$7,284 - 51 =$

A 2,184
B 7,223
C 7,374
D 7,233
E None of these

14

288
− 91

F 297
G 197
H 379
J 97
K None of these

15

$5,584 - 3,211 =$

A 2,373
B 3,273
C 8,795
D 3,377
E None of these

16

$4,365 - 187 =$

F 4,128
G 4,178
H 4,187
J 4,278
K None of these

17

79
− 25

A 45
B 64
C 55
D 53
E None of these

18

341
− 59

F 382
G 318
H 282
J 292
K None of these

Check your answers on pages 50–51.

Lesson 5   Multiplication of Whole Numbers—No Regrouping

Multiplication is the same as repeated addition. For example, if you have a case of juice that has 4 six-packs in it, you can add to find out how many cans of juice you have. $6 + 6 + 6 + 6 = 24$ cans. It is much easier, though, to multiply 4 by 6 to get the answer.

Example Multiply. $4 \times 6 =$

4 six packs = 24 cans
$4 \times 6 = 24$

Example Multiply. $43 \times 12 =$

1. Line up the digits.

```
  tens ones
    4   3
 ×  1   2
```

2. Multiply by 2 ones.
Multiply by 1 ten.

```
      tens ones
        4   3
  ×     1   2
        8   6
    4   3   0
```

3. Add $86 + 430$.

```
 hundreds tens ones
          4   3
  ×       1   2
      1   8   6
  + 4     3   0
    5     1   6
```

$12 \times 43 = 516$

Test Example

Multiply. Circle the answer.

1

    $54 \times 0 =$

    A 0

    B 54

    C 50

    D 1

    E None of these

Hint
When you multiply any number by 0, the answer is 0.

```
1   A     54
        × 0
          0
```

Multiply. Circle the answer.

1

$3 \times 12 =$

A 36
B 15
C 24
D 30
E None of these

6

$\begin{array}{r} 71 \\ \times\ 5 \\ \hline \end{array}$

F 305
G 125
H 356
J 355
K None of these

2

$\begin{array}{r} 80 \\ \times\ 8 \\ \hline \end{array}$

F 880
G 640
H 800
J 168
K None of these

7

$86 \times 0 =$

A 80
B 6
C 0
D 68
E None of these

3

$41 \times 24 =$

A 904
B 246
C 984
D 784
E None of these

8

$13 \times 23 =$

F 300
G 299
H 36
J 65
K None of these

4

$3 \times 320 =$

F 323
G 963
H 653
J 950
K None of these

9

$50 \times 9 =$

A 509
B 500
C 460
D 450
E None of these

5

$20 \times 8 =$

A 100
B 160
C 280
D 180
E None of these

10

$5 \times 11 =$

F 50
G 60
H 55
J 16
K None of these

Check your answers on page 51.

Multiplication of Whole Numbers—Regrouping

You sat in the last seat in the last row in the auditorium for a sold-out concert. You were in seat 43 of row 58. You can use multiplication with regrouping to figure out how many people were at the concert.

Example Multiply. 58 × 43 =

1. Be sure the digits are lined up. Multiply by 3 ones. 3 × 8 = 24 ones. Regroup the 2. 3 × 5 = 15 tens. Add the 2.

```
        1   2
            5   8
    ×       4   3
        1   7   4
```

2. Multiply by 4 tens. 4 × 8 = 32 tens. Regroup the 3. 4 × 5 = 20 hundreds. Add the 3.

```
                3
        1       2
                5   8
    ×           4   3
            1   7   4
    2   3   2   0
```

3. Add 174 + 2,320.

```
            5   8
    ×       4   3
        1   7   4
  + 2   3   2   0
    2   4   9   4
```

Hint

As soon as you've added the regrouped numbers, cross them out to keep from getting confused.

43 × 58 = 2,494. There were 2,494 people at the concert.

Test Example

Multiply. Circle the answer.

1

369 × 24 =

A   8,856

B   8,756

C   7,856

D   7,876

E   None of these

```
1   A        1 1
           1 2 3
             369
         ×    24
           1,476
         + 7,380
           8,856
```

Math Computation

Multiply. Circle the answer.

1

974
× 51

A 46,674
B 49,474
C 48,674
D 49,674
E None of these

2

74
× 16

F 1,148
G 1,164
H 1,384
J 1,184
K None of these

3

744
× 67

A 47,548
B 47,428
C 50,848
D 49,484
E None of these

4

5,921
× 9

F 52,289
G 53,289
H 53,290
J 53,189
K None of these

5

15 × 563 =

A 7,445
B 8,145
C 8,445
D 8,135
E None of these

6

82
× 29

F 2,378
G 2,478
H 2,368
J 1,368
K None of these

7

927
× 58

A 53,764
B 54,966
C 53,766
D 43,766
E None of these

8

392 × 49 =

F 19,208
G 19,198
H 20,208
J 15,398
K None of these

9

2,987
× 4

A 8,628
B 11,948
C 8,948
D 11,648
E None of these

10

257 × 26 =

F 8,682
G 6,882
H 6,982
J 6,642
K None of these

Check your answers on page 51.

Multiply. Circle the answer.

1

$$62 \times 35$$

A 2,170
B 2,270
C 2,160
D 1,170
E None of these

6

$$32 \times 4$$

F 126
G 36
H 76
J 158
K None of these

2

$40 \times 4 =$

F 4
G 0
H 144
J 160
K None of these

7

$21 \times 0 =$

A 21
B 1
C 12
D 0
E None of these

3

$$6,458 \times 5$$

A 30,290
B 32,250
C 30,050
D 32,290
E None of these

8

$3 \times 20 =$

F 23
G 60
H 17
J 66
K None of these

4

$61 \times 13 =$

F 793
G 244
H 733
J 693
K None of these

9

$$379 \times 89$$

A 34,731
B 33,731
C 32,731
D 33,831
E None of these

5

$813 \times 64 =$

A 51,932
B 52,032
C 42,032
D 52,022
E None of these

10

$70 \times 8 =$

F 540
G 708
H 780
J 560
K None of these

11

   91
$\times$ 3

A 237
B 183
C 273
D 284
E None of these

12

$210 \times 5 =$

F 1,050
G 1,005
H 1,550
J 1,500
K None of these

13

  574
$\times$ 36

A 20,764
B 22,664
C 22,764
D 20,664
E None of these

14

  43
$\times$ 17

F 700
G 711
H 731
J 374
K None of these

15

  973
$\times$ 54

A 41,442
B 52,542
C 53,542
D 49,172
E None of these

16

$18 \times 356 =$

F 6,408
G 5,968
H 5,308
J 9,808
K None of these

17

$63 \times 0 =$

A 60
B 1
C 0
D 63
E None of these

18

 7,137
$\times$ 4

F 28,448
G 29,548
H 28,528
J 28,428
K None of these

Check your answers on pages 51–52.

Lesson 7 Division of Whole Numbers—No Remainder

You have to move 180 books and have 9 boxes to pack them in. An easy way to find out how many books you can put into each box is to divide. On the TABE you will see division problems written with a division sign ($180 \div 9$), using a bracket for long division ($9\overline{)180}$), or as a fraction with one number over the other $\left(\frac{180}{9}\right)$.

Example Divide. $180 \div 9 =$

1. Divide. Since you can't divide 1 by 9 evenly, divide 18 by 9. $18 \div 9 = 2$. Write the 2 above the 8. Subtract $18 - 18 = 0$.

$$
\begin{array}{r}
2 \\
9\overline{)180} \\
-18 \\
\hline
0
\end{array}
$$

2. Bring down the next place value. You can't divide 9 into 0, so write 0 above the 0 in the ones place.

$$
\begin{array}{r}
20 \\
9\overline{)180} \\
-18\downarrow \\
\hline
00 \\
-0 \\
\hline
0
\end{array}
$$

$180 \div 9 = 20$. You can put 20 books into each of the 9 boxes.

Test Example

Divide. Circle the answer.

1 $\dfrac{9000}{5} =$

A 1,800

B 9,000

C 6,000

D 400

E None of these

Hint

To check your work, multiply your answer by the number you divided by (5). $1800 \times 5 = 9,000$.

1 A   1,800
$$
\begin{array}{r}
5\overline{)9,000} \\
-5 \\
\hline
40 \\
-40 \\
\hline
000
\end{array}
$$

Practice

Divide. Circle the answer.

1

5)245

A 49
B 48
C 53
D 59
E None of these

2

7,600 ÷ 4 =

F 200
G 190
H 1,800
J 1,900
K None of these

3

99
──
33

A 33
B 3
C 9
D 11
E None of these

4

9)54

F 50
G 60
H 7
J 6
K None of these

5

7)8,981

A 1,238
B 1,273
C 1,353
D 1,383
E None of these

6

5)7,635

F 1,525
G 1,501
H 1,527
J 1,507
K None of these

7

48
──
12 =

A 3
B 40
C 12
D 4
E None of these

8

6)432

F 74
G 71
H 72
J 61
K None of these

9

8,320 ÷ 2 =

A 41
B 416
C 4,060
D 4,110
E None of these

10

6)42

F 7
G 6
H 8
J 2
K None of these

Check your answers on page 52.

Lesson 8   Division of Whole Numbers—Remainder

Sometimes a number won't evenly divide another number. The amount left over is called the *remainder*.

If 9 people want to pair up to play catch, how many teams of 2 can play catch at the same time? Can everyone play catch, or will some have to wait on the bench? You can use division to figure out how many pairs can play and how many people will have to wait.

Example   Divide. 9 ÷ 2 =

1. Rewrite the problem using the division bracket. Put the first number inside the bracket. Put the second number to the left of the bracket.

$$2\overline{)9}$$

2. Find out how many times 2 goes into 9. 2 goes into 9 four times. Write 4 above the bracket. Multiply. $4 \times 2 = 8$. Write 8 below the 9. Subtract. $9 - 8 = 1$.

$$\begin{array}{r} 4 \\ 2\overline{)9} \\ -8 \\ \hline 1 \end{array}$$

3. 2 does not go into 1 and there are no more numbers to bring down so 1 is the remainder. Write the remainder next to the 4 using R1.

$$\begin{array}{r} 4 \text{ R1} \\ 2\overline{)9} \\ -8 \\ \hline 1 \end{array}$$

Hint

To check your work, multiply your answer by 4 and add the remainder.
$4 \times 2 = 8$
$8 + 1 = 9$

$9 \div 2 = 4$ **R1. There will be 4 pairs of people playing catch. One person will remain on the bench.**

Test Example

Divide. Circle the answer.

1   **A** 2 R1

$7 \div 4 =$ **B** 1 R1

          C 1

          D 1 R3

          E None of these

1   D $\begin{array}{r} 1 \text{ R3} \\ 4\overline{)7} \\ -4 \\ \hline 3 \end{array}$

Divide. Circle the answer.

1
9 ÷ 6 =
A 1 R2
B 2
C 1 R3
D 1
E None of these

6
9 ÷ 8 =
F 1 R1
G 1
H 2
J 2 R1
K None of these

2
6)7
F 1 R2
G 1
H 2 R5
J 2
K None of these

7
940 ÷ 6 =
A 156
B 156 R4
C 166
D 166 R4
E None of these

3
5 ÷ 2 =
A 2 R1
B 2
C 3 R1
D 3
E None of these

8
2)7
F 1 R2
G 3 R1
H 4 R1
J 2 R1
K None of these

4
7)15
F 3
G 2 R1
H 2 R7
J 1 R5
K None of these

9
6)8
A 2 R4
B 1
C 1 R2
D 2
E None of these

5
8 ÷ 3 =
A 2
B 2 R1
C 2 R2
D 3
E None of these

10
86 ÷ 40 =
F 2 R4
G 3 R6
H 20 R6
J 23 R6
K None of these

Check your answers on pages 52–53.

Divide. Circle the answer.

1

7,800 ÷ 3 =

   A 2,900
   B 2,600
   C 2,230
   D 3,600
   E None of these

2

7 ÷ 5 =

   F 1
   G 1 R2
   H 2
   J 2 R1
   K None of these

3

$8\overline{)752}$

   A 92
   B 84
   C 86
   D 94
   E None of these

4

80 ÷ 20 =

   F 40
   G 5
   H 4
   J 44
   K None of these

5

$7\overline{)8}$

   A 1 R1
   B 1
   C 2 R6
   D 2
   E None of these

6

$\dfrac{77}{11} =$

   F 77
   G 1
   H 7
   J 11
   K None of these

7

9 ÷ 7 =

   A 1 R1
   B 1
   C 2 R1
   D 2
   E None of these

8

$5\overline{)9}$

   F 2 R1
   G 1 R4
   H 1 R1
   J 1 R3
   K None of these

9

$2\overline{)9,304}$

   A 4,652
   B 4,602
   C 4,552
   D 4,657
   E None of these

10

$8 \div 5 =$

   F 2 R2
   G 1 R3
   H 1
   J 2
   K None of these

11

$3\overline{)27}$

   A 6 R3
   B 8
   C 9 R1
   D 7
   E None of these

12

$8\overline{)64}$

   F 18
   G 8
   H 9
   J 7
   K None of these

13

$\dfrac{80}{10} =$

   A 90
   B 9
   C 8
   D 80
   E None of these

14

$3\overline{)7}$

   F 2 R2
   G 3 R1
   H 2 R1
   J 2 R3
   K None of these

15

$3\overline{)8,652}$

   A 2,884
   B 3,217
   C 2,284
   D 2,864
   E None of these

16

$3\overline{)5}$

   F 1 R1
   G 2 R1
   H 2
   J 1
   K None of these

17

$8,610 \div 7 =$

   A 132
   B 1,130
   C 1,230
   D 123
   E None of these

18 $9\overline{)297}$

   F 30
   G 23
   H 32
   J 31
   K None of these

Check your answers on page 53.

Lesson 9 | Addition of Decimals

While you are doing laundry you find a dollar ($1) in one pocket and a quarter ($0.25) in another pocket. You add to find the total value of the money you have. The decimal $0.25 stands for an amount smaller than a whole dollar. Decimals are numbers written with a decimal point.

Example Add. 1 + .25 =

1. If a whole number doesn't have a decimal point (as with $1), you will need to write a decimal point after the number. Place one number under the other, lining up the decimal points. Make sure both numbers have the same number of digits to the right of the decimal point by adding 0s to the shorter number.

```
  1 . 0   0
+   . 2   5
```

2. Write a decimal point below the answer line so that it lines up with the other decimal points.

```
  1 . 0   0
+   . 2   5
      .
```

3. Add just as if you were adding numbers without decimal points.

```
  1 . 0   0
+   . 2   5
  1 . 2   5
```

1 + .25 = 1.25

Hint

Always line up the decimal points *before* adding to be sure you have the decimal point in the correct place in the answer.

Test Example

Add. Circle the answer.

1

23 + 5.6 =

A   7.9

B   28.6

C   23.56

D   5.83

E   None of these

```
1  B    23.0
      +  5.6
        28.6
```

Add. Circle the answer.

1

$$\begin{array}{r} 73 \\ + \ 2.4 \\ \hline \end{array}$$

A 97
B 75.04
C 75.4
D 9.7
E None of these

2 12 + 4.2 =

F 5.4
G 12.42
H 4.32
J 16.2
K None of these

3 25 + 4.1

A 29.1
B 25.4
C 26.0
D 21.1
E None of these

4

$$\begin{array}{r} 4.5 \\ + \ 3.4 \\ \hline \end{array}$$

F 7.09
G 8.89
H 4.3
J 1.9
K None of these

5 34 + 3.1 =

A 34.31
B 6.5
C 37.1
D 3.54
E None of these

6 4.2 + 3 =

F 6.7
G 7.2
H 42.3
J 1.2
K None of these

7

$$\begin{array}{r} 62 \\ + \ 3.7 \\ \hline \end{array}$$

A 65.7
B 10.9
C 65.07
D 62.37
E None of these

8 2 + 4.7 =

F 24.17
G 6.17
H 6.7
J 42.7
K None of these

9 42 + 6.9 =

A 42.69
B 49.9
C 7.32
D 11.1
E None of these

10

$$\begin{array}{r} 5.3 \\ + \ 3 \\ \hline \end{array}$$

F 7.9
G 2.3
H 6.0
J 8.3
K None of these

Check your answers on pages 53–54.

Lesson 10 Subtraction of Decimals

Subtracting decimal numbers is much like subtracting numbers without decimals. You just have to be sure to line up the decimal points before you begin to subtract.

Example 29.4 − 0.65 =

1. Place the greater number over the lesser number, lining up the decimal points. Make sure that both numbers have the same number of digits to the right of the decimal point by adding 0 to the shorter number.

$$
\begin{array}{r}
2\ 9\ .\ 4\ \mathbf{0} \\
-\quad 0\ .\ 6\ 5 \\
\hline
\end{array}
$$

2. Write a decimal point in the answer line so that it lines up under the other decimal points. Subtract starting with the hundredths. You can't take 5 away from 0, so take $\frac{1}{10}$ away from the tenths place. Regroup, then subtract. 10 − 5 = 5.

$$
\begin{array}{r}
{}^{3}\ {}^{10} \\
2\ 9\ .\ \cancel{4}\ \cancel{0} \\
-\quad 0\ .\ 6\ \mathbf{5} \\
\hline
.\quad\ \ \mathbf{5}
\end{array}
$$

3. You now have 3 tenths instead of 4. You can't take 6 away from 3, so regroup again. Take 1 from the ones column, change it to 10 tenths, and add it to the tenths column. Subtract 13 − 6 = 7.

$$
\begin{array}{r}
{}^{8}\quad {}^{13} \\
\quad {}^{\cancel{3}}\ {}^{10} \\
2\ \cancel{9}\ .\ \cancel{4}\ \cancel{0} \\
-\quad 0\ .\ 6\ 5 \\
\hline
.\ \mathbf{7}\ \mathbf{5}
\end{array}
$$

4. Subtract the ones. You now have 8 ones because you regrouped. 8 − 0 = 8. Write 8 below the 0 in the ones column. Bring down the 2 in the tens column, since there is nothing to subtract from it.

$$
\begin{array}{r}
{}^{8}\quad {}^{13} \\
\quad {}^{\cancel{3}}\ {}^{10} \\
2\ \cancel{9}\ .\ \cancel{4}\ \cancel{0} \\
-\quad \mathbf{0}\ .\ 6\ 5 \\
\hline
\mathbf{2}\ \mathbf{8}\ .\ 7\ 5
\end{array}
$$

29.4 − 0.65 = 28.75

Test Example

Subtract. Circle the answer.

1
  64.2 − 0.61 =

   A 64.59

   B 64.41

   C 63.59

   D 63.61

   E None of these

$$
\begin{array}{r}
{}^{3}\ {}^{11} \\
\quad {}^{\cancel{1}\ 10} \\
1\quad C\quad 64.2\cancel{0} \\
-\ \ 0.61 \\
\hline
63.59
\end{array}
$$

Subtract. Circle the answer.

1

$$52.4 - 0.76$$

A 51.64
B 52.36
C 52.44
D 51.76
E None of these

2

$36.0 - 3.526 =$

F 33.526
G 33.474
H 32.474
J 32.586
K None of these

3

$13.4 - 0.56 =$

A 13.16
B 12.96
C 13.84
D 12.84
E None of these

4

$18.0 - 5.719 =$

F 13.719
G 13.281
H 12.28
J 12.31
K None of these

5

$$15.3 - .73$$

A 13.57
B 12.63
C 14.57
D 13.43
E None of these

6

$94.0 - 6.759 =$

F 87.241
G 87.359
H 92.759
J 88.241
K None of these

7

$57.9 - 0.93 =$

A 57.97
B 56.97
C 56.07
D 57.03
E None of these

8

$82.0 - 4.672 =$

F 77.472
G 76.328
H 87.327
J 82.672
K None of these

9

$$44.2 - 0.81$$

A 44.61
B 43.41
C 43.39
D 44.39
E None of these

10

$$75.0 - 3.72$$

F 71.72
G 71.28
H 72.68
J 73.72
K None of these

Check your answers on page 54.

Multiplication of Decimals

Multiplication of decimals is just like multiplication of whole numbers, except that you have to know how to place the decimal point in the answer.

Example Multiply. $3.4 \times 0.6 =$

1. Place one number under the other. Line up the numbers at the right, not by decimal points.

$$
\begin{array}{r}
3.4 \\
\times\,0.6 \\
\hline
\end{array}
$$

2. Multiply starting from the right. $6 \times 4 = 24$. Write 4 below the 6 and regroup the 2, placing it above the 3. Don't include a decimal point yet.

$$
\begin{array}{r}
\overset{2}{}3.4 \\
\times\,0.6 \\
\hline
4
\end{array}
$$

3. Multiply the 6 by the 3. $6 \times 3 = 18$. Now add the regrouped number, 2. $18 + 2 = 20$. Write 20 below the line.

$$
\begin{array}{r}
\overset{2}{3}.4 \\
\times\,0.6 \\
\hline
2\,0\,4
\end{array}
$$

4. To put the decimal in the proper place, count places to the right of the decimal point in both 3.4 and 0.6. Add the number of places to find out how many decimal places the answer should have. There is one digit after the decimal point in each number. $1 + 1 = 2$. The decimal point goes 2 digits from the right.

$$
\begin{array}{r}
3.4 \quad \rightarrow \quad \text{1 decimal place} \\
\times\,0.6 \quad \leftarrow \quad +\text{ 1 decimal place} \\
\hline
2.0\,4 \quad \text{2 decimal places}
\end{array}
$$

$3.4 \times 0.6 = 2.04$

Test Example

Multiply. Circle the answer.

1

$0.374 \times 400 =$

A 1,496.0

B   1.496

C   14.96

D   149.6

E   None of these

1 D
$$
\begin{array}{r}
\overset{2\,1}{}0.374 \\
\times\quad 400 \\
\hline
149.600
\end{array}
$$

Practice

Multiply. Circle the answer.

1

$0.7 \times 3 =$

- A   2.1
- B   0.21
- C   0.021
- D   21.0
- E   None of these

2

$0.752 \times 500 =$

- F   376.0
- G   0.376
- H   3.76
- J   37.6
- K   None of these

3

$784.6 \times 0.7 =$

- A   49.682
- B   549.22
- C   496.82
- D   54.922
- E   None of these

4

$\begin{array}{r} 6 \\ \times\, 0.6 \\ \hline \end{array}$

- F   0.36
- G   36.0
- H   3.6
- J   3.06
- K   None of these

5

$\begin{array}{r} 3.8 \\ \times\, 1.9 \\ \hline \end{array}$

- A   722.0
- B   72.2
- C   65.2
- D   6.52
- E   None of these

6

$562.1 \times 0.9 =$

- F   50.589
- G   454.89
- H   45.489
- J   455.89
- K   None of these

7

$0.469 \times 300 =$

- A   14.07
- B   1.407
- C   140.7
- D   1,407.0
- E   None of these

8

$0.4 \times 7 =$

- F   28.0
- G   0.028
- H   0.28
- J   2.8
- K   None of these

9

$\begin{array}{r} 6.7 \\ \times\, 8.4 \\ \hline \end{array}$

- A   56.28
- B   562.8
- C   51.08
- D   510.8
- E   None of these

10

$\begin{array}{r} 8 \\ \times\, 0.6 \\ \hline \end{array}$

- F   48.0
- G   4.8
- H   0.48
- J   4.08
- K   None of these

Check your answers on page 54.

1

$$\begin{array}{r} 14.6 \\ - 0.35 \\ \hline \end{array}$$

- **A** 14.24
- **B** 13.35
- **C** 14.35
- **D** 13.25
- **E** None of these

2

$351.7 \times 0.4 =$

- **F** 1,406.8
- **G** 120.48
- **H** 140.68
- **J** 12.048
- **K** None of these

3

$21 + 2.3 =$

- **A** 23.3
- **B** 22.3
- **C** 21.2
- **D** 21.3
- **E** None of these

4

$$\begin{array}{r} 37.6 \\ - 0.34 \\ \hline \end{array}$$

- **F** 37.34
- **G** 37.26
- **H** 37.36
- **J** 36.36
- **K** None of these

5

$$\begin{array}{r} 7 \\ \times 0.9 \\ \hline \end{array}$$

- **A** 6.3
- **B** 63.0
- **C** 0.63
- **D** 0.603
- **E** None of these

6

$$\begin{array}{r} 81 \\ + 1.6 \\ \hline \end{array}$$

- **F** 81.16
- **G** 82.06
- **H** 97
- **J** 82.6
- **K** None of these

7

$72.3 - 0.41 =$

- **A** 72.11
- **B** 72.89
- **C** 71.89
- **D** 71.91
- **E** None of these

8

$0.819 \times 600 =$

- **F** 4,914.0
- **G** 419.4
- **H** 4.914
- **J** 49.14
- **K** None of these

9

$53.0 - 1.245 =$

- **A** 51.845
- **B** 52.245
- **C** 51.755
- **D** 52.755
- **E** None of these

10

$6.4 + 2 =$

F 6.8
G 8.4
H 6.62
J 8.8
K None of these

11

$0.5 \times 9 =$

A 0.045
B 45.0
C 0.45
D 4.5
E None of these

12

$\begin{array}{r} 13.0 \\ + .67 \\ \hline \end{array}$

F 80.0
G 13.77
H 13.67
J 19.67
K None of these

13

$45.0 - 2.741 =$

A 43.741
B 42.258
C 43.259
D 42.259
E None of these

14

$6 + 3.1 =$

F 9.7
G 6.31
H 7.3
J 10.1
K None of these

15

$\begin{array}{r} 23.5 \\ - .34 \\ \hline \end{array}$

A 23.16
B 22.24
C 23.26
D 21.16
E None of these

16

$\begin{array}{r} 9.2 \\ \times 7.5 \\ \hline \end{array}$

F 67.9
G 679.0
H 690.0
J 69.00
K None of these

17

$51 + 8.4 =$

A 13.5
B 59.4
C 51.84
D 8.91
E None of these

18

$\begin{array}{r} 5 \\ \times 0.8 \\ \hline \end{array}$

F 0.4
G 4.0
H 40.0
J 4.5
K None of these

Check your answers on pages 54–55.

Lesson 12 › Addition of Fractions

A fraction is a number that names a part of a whole. For example, there are 4 quarts in 1 gallon, so 1 quart would be $\frac{1}{4}$ of a gallon. If you had 2 quarts, or $\frac{1}{4}$ gallon + $\frac{1}{4}$ gallon, you'd have $\frac{2}{4}$ gallon, or $\frac{1}{2}$ gallon. On the TABE, you will be asked to add fractions.

Example Add.
$$\frac{1}{6}$$
$$+\frac{2}{6}$$

1. Write out the problem in horizontal form. Because both fractions have the same bottom number, 6, the bottom number of the answer will also be 6. Write 6 under the fraction bar.

$$\frac{1}{6} + \frac{2}{6} = \frac{}{6}$$

2. Add the top numbers. Write 3 above the fraction bar.

$$\frac{1}{6} + \frac{2}{6} = \frac{3}{6}$$

3. Reduce the answer to its lowest terms. Divide both the top number, 3, and the bottom number, 6, by a number that divides evenly into both.

$$\frac{3}{6} \div \frac{3}{3} = \frac{1}{2}$$

Because no other number evenly divides both 1 and 2, $\frac{1}{2}$ is in its lowest terms.

$$\frac{1}{6} + \frac{2}{6} = \frac{1}{2}$$

Test Example

Add. Circle the answer.

1
$$\frac{5}{7}$$
$$+\frac{3}{7}$$

A $1\frac{2}{7}$

B $\frac{5}{6}$

C $\frac{4}{7}$

D $1\frac{1}{7}$

E None of these

Hint

Make sure the fraction is in its lowest terms before choosing *None of these*.

1 D $\frac{5}{7} + \frac{3}{7} = \frac{8}{7} = 1\frac{1}{7}$

Add. Circle the answer.

1 $\frac{3}{5}$
$+\frac{1}{5}$

A $\frac{2}{5}$

B $\frac{3}{10}$

C $1\frac{1}{5}$

D $\frac{4}{5}$

E None of these

2 $\frac{3}{4}$
$+\frac{3}{4}$

F $\frac{6}{7}$

G $1\frac{1}{2}$

H $1\frac{1}{4}$

J $\frac{3}{4}$

K None of these

3 $\frac{5}{6}$
$+\frac{4}{6}$

A $1\frac{1}{2}$

B 3

C $1\frac{1}{3}$

D $\frac{5}{6}$

E None of these

4 $\frac{3}{9}$
$+\frac{4}{9}$

F $\frac{7}{9}$

G $\frac{8}{9}$

H $\frac{7}{18}$

J $\frac{2}{3}$

K None of these

5 $\frac{5}{8}$
$+\frac{7}{8}$

A $1\frac{1}{4}$

B $\frac{3}{4}$

C $1\frac{1}{2}$

D $1\frac{3}{8}$

E None of these

6 $\frac{5}{9}$
$+\frac{1}{9}$

F $\frac{1}{3}$

G $\frac{6}{18}$

H $\frac{7}{9}$

J $\frac{5}{9}$

K None of these

7 $\frac{2}{4}$
$+\frac{1}{4}$

A $\frac{3}{8}$

B $\frac{1}{2}$

C $\frac{1}{8}$

D $\frac{3}{4}$

E None of these

8 $\frac{2}{5}$
$+\frac{3}{5}$

F $1\frac{1}{5}$

G 1

H $\frac{4}{5}$

J $\frac{1}{2}$

K None of these

9 $\frac{3}{6}$
$+\frac{1}{6}$

A $\frac{5}{6}$

B $\frac{1}{12}$

C $\frac{2}{3}$

D $\frac{1}{2}$

E None of these

10 $\frac{8}{9}$
$+\frac{5}{9}$

F $1\frac{1}{3}$

G $1\frac{5}{9}$

H $\frac{13}{18}$

J $\frac{9}{13}$

K None of these

Check your answers on page 55.

Lesson 13 | Subtraction of Fractions

The rules for subtracting fractions are the same as the rules for adding fractions. If the bottom number in each fraction is the same, the bottom number of the answer will be the same. Subtract only the top numbers.

Example Subtract. $\dfrac{9}{10}$

$-\dfrac{4}{10}$

1. Write out the problem in horizontal form, adding an equal sign (=) and a fraction bar (—).

$$\frac{9}{10} - \frac{4}{10} = \overline{}$$

2. Look at the bottom numbers. Because both fractions have the same bottom number, 10, the bottom number of the answer will also be 10. Write 10 under the fraction bar.

$$\frac{9}{10} - \frac{4}{10} = \frac{}{10}$$

3. Subtract the top numbers. (9 − 4 = 5) Write 5 above the fraction bar.

$$\frac{9}{10} - \frac{4}{10} = \frac{5}{10}$$

$$\frac{9}{10} - \frac{4}{10} = \frac{1}{2}$$

4. Reduce the answer to its lowest terms. You can evenly divide the top and bottom numbers by 5. (5 ÷ 5 = 1, 10 ÷ 5 = 2)

$$\frac{5}{10} \div \frac{5}{5} = \frac{1}{2}$$

Test Example

Subtract. Circle the answer.

1 $\dfrac{14}{17}$

$-\dfrac{5}{17}$

A $\dfrac{9}{17}$

B $1\dfrac{1}{2}$

C $1\dfrac{2}{17}$

D $1\dfrac{1}{17}$

E None of these

1 A $\dfrac{14}{17} - \dfrac{5}{17} = \dfrac{9}{17}$

Math Computation

Subtract. Circle the answer.

1. $\dfrac{15}{21}$
$-\dfrac{12}{21}$

  A $1\dfrac{1}{3}$

  B $\dfrac{4}{21}$

  C $\dfrac{1}{7}$

  D $\dfrac{1}{6}$

  E   None of these

2. $\dfrac{5}{6} - \dfrac{1}{6} =$

  F $\dfrac{1}{3}$

  G $\dfrac{3}{4}$

  H 1

  J $\dfrac{2}{3}$

  K   None of these

3. $\dfrac{6}{8} - \dfrac{4}{8} =$

  A $1\dfrac{1}{4}$

  B $\dfrac{1}{2}$

  C $1\dfrac{1}{8}$

  D $\dfrac{1}{5}$

  E   None of these

4. $\dfrac{19}{34}$
$-\dfrac{11}{34}$

  F $\dfrac{15}{17}$

  G $\dfrac{4}{17}$

  H $\dfrac{9}{34}$

  J $\dfrac{1}{4}$

  K   None of these

5. $\dfrac{6}{7} - \dfrac{5}{7} =$

  A $\dfrac{2}{7}$

  B $1\dfrac{4}{7}$

  C $1\dfrac{5}{7}$

  D $\dfrac{1}{7}$

  E   None of these

6. $\dfrac{26}{27}$
$-\dfrac{8}{27}$

  F $\dfrac{3}{4}$

  G $1\dfrac{1}{3}$

  H $\dfrac{19}{27}$

  J $\dfrac{1}{3}$

  K   None of these

7. $\dfrac{8}{11} - \dfrac{2}{11} =$

  A $\dfrac{1}{2}$

  B $\dfrac{10}{11}$

  C $\dfrac{6}{11}$

  D $\dfrac{3}{5}$

  E   None of these

8. $\dfrac{21}{30}$
$-\dfrac{6}{30}$

  F $\dfrac{2}{3}$

  G $\dfrac{8}{15}$

  H $\dfrac{17}{30}$

  J $\dfrac{1}{2}$

  K   None of these

9. $\dfrac{4}{5} - \dfrac{4}{5} =$

  A $\dfrac{1}{5}$

  B 0

  C $\dfrac{4}{5}$

  D 1

  E   None of these

10. $\dfrac{12}{18}$
$-\dfrac{8}{18}$

  F $1\dfrac{1}{9}$

  G $\dfrac{2}{9}$

  H $\dfrac{5}{18}$

  J $\dfrac{2}{8}$

  K   None of these

Check your answers on pages 55–56.

Solve. Circle the answer.

1 $\dfrac{7}{15}$
    $-\dfrac{3}{15}$

    A $\dfrac{2}{3}$
    B $\dfrac{1}{5}$
    C $\dfrac{1}{3}$
    D $\dfrac{4}{15}$
    E None of these

5 $\dfrac{3}{6}$
    $+\dfrac{4}{6}$

    A $\dfrac{6}{7}$
    B $1\dfrac{1}{6}$
    C $1\dfrac{1}{3}$
    D $\dfrac{7}{12}$
    E None of these

2 $\dfrac{7}{12}+\dfrac{3}{12}=$

    F $\dfrac{10}{24}$
    G $\dfrac{5}{6}$
    H $\dfrac{11}{12}$
    J $\dfrac{3}{4}$
    K None of these

6 $\dfrac{6}{8}-\dfrac{3}{8}=$

    F $\dfrac{1}{2}$
    G $\dfrac{1}{3}$
    H $\dfrac{3}{8}$
    J $\dfrac{5}{8}$
    K None of these

3 $\dfrac{5}{7}$
    $+\dfrac{1}{7}$

    A $\dfrac{5}{14}$
    B $\dfrac{6}{7}$
    C $\dfrac{4}{7}$
    D $\dfrac{3}{7}$
    E None of these

7 $\dfrac{7}{9}-\dfrac{1}{9}=$

    A $\dfrac{2}{3}$
    B $\dfrac{3}{4}$
    C $\dfrac{8}{9}$
    D $\dfrac{5}{9}$
    E None of these

4 $\dfrac{10}{15}-\dfrac{7}{15}=$

    F $\dfrac{2}{15}$
    G $\dfrac{1}{3}$
    H $\dfrac{4}{15}$
    J $\dfrac{1}{5}$
    K None of these

8 $\dfrac{2}{4}$
    $+\dfrac{3}{4}$

    F $1\dfrac{1}{2}$
    G $\dfrac{5}{8}$
    H $1\dfrac{1}{4}$
    J $\dfrac{3}{4}$
    K None of these

9

$$\frac{8}{9} - \frac{5}{9} =$$

A $\frac{1}{9}$

B $\frac{1}{3}$

C $\frac{4}{9}$

D $\frac{2}{3}$

E None of these

13

$$\frac{3}{7}$$
$$+\frac{2}{7}$$

A $\frac{5}{7}$

B $\frac{1}{7}$

C $\frac{6}{7}$

D $\frac{5}{14}$

E None of these

10

$$\frac{7}{9}$$
$$+\frac{8}{9}$$

F $1\frac{5}{9}$

G $1\frac{2}{3}$

H $1\frac{5}{6}$

J $1\frac{7}{9}$

K None of these

14

$$\frac{6}{20} + \frac{5}{20} + \frac{4}{20} =$$

F $\frac{1}{4}$

G $\frac{13}{20}$

H $\frac{15}{60}$

J $\frac{3}{4}$

K None of these

11

$$\frac{7}{10}$$
$$-\frac{3}{10}$$

A $\frac{1}{5}$

B $\frac{2}{10}$

C $\frac{3}{10}$

D $\frac{1}{2}$

E None of these

15

$$\frac{4}{8}$$
$$+\frac{1}{8}$$

A $\frac{5}{6}$

B $\frac{5}{8}$

C $\frac{1}{2}$

D $\frac{3}{8}$

E None of these

12

$$\frac{20}{24}$$
$$-\frac{8}{24}$$

F $\frac{7}{12}$

G $1\frac{1}{6}$

H $\frac{1}{2}$

J $\frac{13}{24}$

K None of these

16

$$\frac{10}{11}$$
$$-\frac{9}{11}$$

F $\frac{1}{11}$

G 1

H $\frac{2}{11}$

J 0

K None of these

Check your answers on page 56.

The Math Computation Performance Assessment is identical to the actual TABE in format and length. It will give you an idea of what the real test is like. Allow yourself 15 minutes to complete this assessment. Check your answers on pages 56–57.

Sample A

Subtract.

239
− 42

A 197

B 297

C 121

D 225

E None of these

1

654 + 43 =

A 1,074

B 697

C 224

D 1,084

E None of these

2

$\frac{39}{13} =$

F 30

G 3

H 10

J 33

K None of these

3

61 × 13 =

A 733

B 244

C 793

D 693

E None of these

4

8 + 7 + 6 =

F 21

G 23

H 13

J 15

K None of these

5

6)̄36

A 13

B 6

C 5

D 3

E None of these

6

357
− 29

F 338

G 332

H 386

J 327

K None of these

TABE Fundamentals: Math Computation

7

$813 \times 64 =$

A 51,932
B 52,032
C 42,032
D 52,022
E None of these

8

$2,824 - 734 =$

F 2,890
G 2,790
H 2,090
J 2,710
K None of these

9

$1,641 - 568 =$

A 1,063
B 1,172
C 1,572
D 1,163
E None of these

10

$$\begin{array}{r} 589 \\ - 244 \end{array}$$

F 355
G 345
H 344
J 354
K None of these

11

$210 \times 5 =$

A 1,500
B 1,005
C 1,050
D 1,550
E None of these

12

$$\begin{array}{r} 2.3 \\ \times 5.1 \end{array}$$

F 107.3
G 117.3
H 11.73
J 10.73
K None of these

13

$0.653 \times 700 =$

A 4.571
B 457.1
C 45.71
D 4,571.0
E None of these

14

$$\begin{array}{r} 27.1 \\ - 0.47 \end{array}$$

F 27.37
G 26.77
H 27.63
J 26.63
K None of these

15

$$\begin{array}{r} \frac{2}{5} \\ + \frac{1}{5} \end{array}$$

A $\frac{3}{5}$
B $\frac{4}{5}$
C $\frac{3}{10}$
D $\frac{1}{5}$
E None of these

16

$356 + 527 =$

F 873
G 882
H 782
J 973
K None of these

17

$5\overline{)7}$

    A 2 R1
    B 1
    C 1 R2
    D 2
    E None of these

22

$21 \times 0 =$

    F 21
    G 10
    H 12
    J 20
    K None of these

18

$\dfrac{11}{12} - \dfrac{3}{12} =$

    F $\dfrac{1}{4}$
    G $\dfrac{1}{3}$
    H $\dfrac{1}{2}$
    J $\dfrac{2}{3}$
    K None of these

23

$\dfrac{7}{8}$
$+ \dfrac{3}{8}$

    A $1\dfrac{3}{4}$
    B $1\dfrac{1}{8}$
    C $\dfrac{5}{8}$
    D $1\dfrac{3}{8}$
    E None of these

19

$6\overline{)3,702}$

    A 607
    B 617
    C 902
    D 917
    E None of these

24

62
$\times 35$

    F 2,170
    G 2,270
    H 2,160
    J 1,170
    K None of these

20

$9,423 + 7 =$

    F 9,431
    G 9,429
    H 9,420
    J 9,430
    K None of these

25

$\dfrac{9}{14}$
$- \dfrac{5}{14}$

    A $\dfrac{2}{7}$
    B $\dfrac{4}{7}$
    C $\dfrac{3}{14}$
    D $\dfrac{13}{14}$
    E None of these

21

$63.0 - 1.756 =$

    A 61.244
    B 62.244
    C 61.356
    D 62.756
    E None of these

STOP

Lesson 1 Practice (page 9)

1. D   6,113
     + 3,476
     9,589

2. K   924
     + 63
      987

3. E   41
      103
      2,100
     + 304
      2,548

4. J   2,941
     + 6,058
     8,999

5. A   102
      510
       27
     + 1,020
      1,659

6. J   637
     + 21
      658

7. B   734
     + 32
      766

8. K   5,871
     + 4,103
     9,974

9. C   360
      3,006
       11
     + 202
      3,579

10. F   1,352
     + 7,506
     8,858

Lesson 2 Practice (page 11)

1. E   582
     + 245
      827

2. G   7,528
     +   7
     7,535

3. C   7
       6
     + 3
      16

4. F   7
     + 9,628
     9,635

5. C   5
       9
     + 6
      20

6. K   9
     + 4,887
     4,896

7. D   738
     + 143
      881

8. F   892
     +   9
      901

9. D   6
     + 5,256
     5,262

10. K   863
     +   9
      872

TABE Review: Addition of Whole Numbers (pages 12–13)

1. E   5,876   [Regrouping]
     +   6
     5,882

2. G   654   [No regrouping]
     + 43
      697

3. B   6,584   [Regrouping]
     +   8
     6,592

4. F   5,001   [No regrouping]
       12
      250
     + 104
     5,367

5. C   684   [Regrouping]
     +   9
      693

6. J   9,423   [Regrouping]
     +   7
     9,430

7. C   295   [Regrouping]
     + 433
      728

8. J   4,952   [Regrouping]
     +   9
     4,961

9. E   356   [Regrouping]
     + 527
      883

10. H   451   [No regrouping]
     + 34
      485

11. E   444   [Regrouping]
     + 657
     1,101

12. G   106   [No regrouping]
          50
        230
   + 1,602
    1,988

13. B   ¹5   [Regrouping]
      8
   + 4
    17

14. H   4,472 [No regrouping]
   + 1,223
    5,695

15. E   ¹¹297 [Regrouping]
   + 333
    630

16. G   ¹¹596 [Regrouping]
   +   7
   603

17. A   ²8 [Regrouping]
    7
  + 6
   21

18. G   6,213 [No regrouping]
   + 1,756
    7,969

Lesson 3 Practice (page 15)

1. D   93
   − 72
    21

2. G   5,671
   −   40
    5,631

3. A   56
   − 22
    34

4. G   7,625
   − 2,404
    5,221

5. A   957
   − 231
    726

---

6. G   9,380
   −   20
    9,360

7. E   4,937
   − 2,413
    2,524

8. H   491
   − 180
    311

9. C   86
   − 41
    45

10. J   761
   − 521
    240

Lesson 4 Practice (page 17)

1. A   ^{7 11}78X
   −   29
    752

2. H   ¹³_{0 3}15Ⅹ
   −   97
    48

3. A   ^{5 14}7,649
   −   477
    7,172

4. J   ^{4 17}_{7 14}2,584
   −   399
    2,185

5. C   ^{2 13}335
   −   41
    294

6. K   ^{4 11}_{1 15}5,259
   −   867
    4,392

7. B   ¹²_{0 2}13X
   −   48
    83

---

8. F   ^{7 14}84X
   −   62
    787

9. A   ^{7 1261}8,27X
   −   643
    7,628

10. F   ⁴¹¹6,518
   −   471
    6,047

TABE Review: Subtraction of Whole Numbers (pages 18–19)

1. E   ^{4 17}35X [Regrouping]
   −   29
    328

2. G   67   [No regrouping]
   − 54
    13

3. D   ^{4 11}518 [Regrouping]
   −   97
    421

4. F   4,919 [No regrouping]
   −   16
    4,903

5. E   ^{5 13}_{3 11}1,64X [Regrouping]
   −   568
    1,073

6. F   853 [No regrouping]
   − 150
    703

7. D   2,961 [No regrouping]
   − 1,710
    1,251

8. K   ^{5 12}627 [Regrouping]
   −   56
    571

9. E   6,558 [No regrouping]
   −   24
    6,534

10. H   8,249   [No regrouping]
  − 7,206
   1,043

11. B   589   [No regrouping]
  − 244
   345

12. J   ⁸ ¹⁴
  9,461   [Regrouping]
  −   520
   8,941

13. D   7,284   [No regrouping]
  −   51
   7,233

14. G   ¹ ¹⁸
  288   [Regrouping]
  − 91
   197

15. A   5,584   [No regrouping]
  − 3,211
   2,373

16. G   ² ¹⁵
   ⁵ ¹⁵
  4,365   [Regrouping]
  −   187
   4,178

17. E   79   [No regrouping]
  − 25
   54

18. H   ² ¹³
   ³ ¹¹
  3 4 1   [Regrouping]
  − 5 9
   2 8 2

Lesson 5 Practice (page 21)

1. A   12
  × 3
   36

2. G   80
  × 8
  640

3. C   41
  × 24
   164
  + 820
   984

4. K   320
  ×   3
   960

5. B   20
  × 8
  160

6. J   71
  × 5
  355

7. C   86
  × 0
   0

8. G   23
  × 13
   69
  + 230
   299

9. D   50
  × 9
  450

10. H   11
  × 5
  55

Lesson 6 Practice (page 23)

1. D   ³²
  974
  × 51
  ¹ 974
  + 48,700
   49,674

2. J   ²
  74
  × 16
  ¹444
  + 740
   1,184

3. E   ² ²
   ³²
  744
  × 67
  5,208
  + 44,640
   49,848

4. G   ⁸ ¹
  5,921
  ×   9
   53,289

5. C   ³¹
  563
  × 15
  ¹
  2,815
  + 5,630
   8,445

6. F   ¹
  82
  × 29
  ¹ 738
  + 1,640
   2,378

7. C   ¹ ³
   ² ⁵
  927
  ×   58
  ₁7,416
  + 46,350
   53,766

8. F   ³
   ⁸ ¹
  392
  × 49
  ¹ ¹
  3,528
  + 15,680
   19,208

9. B   ³ ³²
  2,987
  ×   4
   11,948

10. K   ¹ ¹
   ³ ⁴
  257
  × 26
  1,542
  + 5,140
   6,682

TABE Review: Multiplication of Whole Numbers (pages 24–25)

1. A   ¹
  62   [Multiplication of
  × 35   Whole Numbers—
  ₁ 310   Regrouping]
  + 1,860
   2,170

2. J   40   [Multiplication of
  × 4   Whole Numbers—
  160   No Regrouping]

3. D   ² ² ⁴
  6,458   [Multiplication of
  ×   5   Whole Numbers—
  32,290   Regrouping]

4. F
$$\begin{array}{r} 61 \\ \times\ 13 \\ \hline 183 \\ +\ 610 \\ \hline 793 \end{array}$$
[Multiplication of Whole Numbers— No Regrouping]

5. B
$$\begin{array}{r} \overset{1}{\overset{1}{}}813 \\ \times\ 64 \\ \hline \overset{1\ 1\ 1}{3{,}252} \\ +\ 48{,}780 \\ \hline 52{,}032 \end{array}$$
[Multiplication of Whole Numbers— Regrouping]

6. K
$$\begin{array}{r} 32 \\ \times\ 4 \\ \hline 128 \end{array}$$
[Multiplication of Whole Numbers— No Regrouping]

7. D
$$\begin{array}{r} 21 \\ \times\ 0 \\ \hline 0 \end{array}$$
[Multiplication of Whole Numbers— No Regrouping]

8. G
$$\begin{array}{r} 20 \\ \times\ 3 \\ \hline 60 \end{array}$$
[Multiplication of Whole Numbers— No Regrouping]

9. B
$$\begin{array}{r} \overset{6\ 7}{\overset{7\ 8}{379}} \\ \times\ 89 \\ \hline 3{,}411 \\ +\ 30{,}320 \\ \hline 33{,}731 \end{array}$$
[Multiplication of Whole Numbers— Regrouping]

10. J
$$\begin{array}{r} 70 \\ \times\ 8 \\ \hline 560 \end{array}$$
[Multiplication of Whole Numbers— No Regrouping]

11. C
$$\begin{array}{r} 91 \\ \times\ 3 \\ \hline 273 \end{array}$$
[Multiplication of Whole Numbers— No Regrouping]

12. F
$$\begin{array}{r} 210 \\ \times\ 5 \\ \hline 1{,}050 \end{array}$$
[Multiplication of Whole Numbers— No Regrouping]

13. D
$$\begin{array}{r} \overset{2\ 1}{\overset{4\ 2}{574}} \\ \times\ 36 \\ \hline 3{,}444 \\ +\ 17{,}220 \\ \hline 20{,}664 \end{array}$$
[Multiplication of Whole Numbers— Regrouping]

14. H
$$\begin{array}{r} \overset{2}{}43 \\ \times\ 17 \\ \hline 301 \\ +\ 430 \\ \hline 731 \end{array}$$
[Multiplication of Whole Numbers— Regrouping]

15. B
$$\begin{array}{r} \overset{3\,1}{\overset{2\,1}{973}} \\ \times\ 54 \\ \hline \overset{1\,1\ 1}{3{,}892} \\ +\ 48{,}650 \\ \hline 52{,}542 \end{array}$$
[Multiplication of Whole Numbers— Regrouping]

16. F
$$\begin{array}{r} \overset{4\ 4}{356} \\ \times\ 18 \\ \hline \overset{1\ 1}{2{,}848} \\ +\ 3{,}560 \\ \hline 6{,}408 \end{array}$$
[Multiplication of Whole Numbers— Regrouping]

17. C
$$\begin{array}{r} 63 \\ \times\ 0 \\ \hline 0 \end{array}$$
[Multiplication of Whole Numbers— No Regrouping]

18. K
$$\begin{array}{r} \overset{1\,2}{7{,}137} \\ \times\ 4 \\ \hline 28{,}548 \end{array}$$
[Multiplication of Whole Numbers— Regrouping]

Lesson 7 Practice (page 27)

1. A
$$\begin{array}{r} 49 \\ 5\overline{)245} \\ -\ 20 \\ \hline 45 \\ -\ 45 \\ \hline 0 \end{array}$$

2. J
$$\begin{array}{r} 1{,}900 \\ 4\overline{)7{,}600} \\ -\ 4 \\ \hline 36 \\ -\ 36 \\ \hline 000 \end{array}$$

3. B
$$\begin{array}{r} 3 \\ 33\overline{)99} \\ -\ 99 \\ \hline 0 \end{array}$$

4. J
$$\begin{array}{r} 6 \\ 9\overline{)54} \\ -\ 54 \\ \hline 0 \end{array}$$

5. E
$$\begin{array}{r} 1{,}283 \\ 7\overline{)8{,}981} \\ -\ 7 \\ \hline 19 \\ -\ 14 \\ \hline 58 \\ -\ 56 \\ \hline 21 \\ -\ 21 \\ \hline 0 \end{array}$$

6. H
$$\begin{array}{r} 1{,}527 \\ 5\overline{)7{,}635} \\ -\ 5 \\ \hline 26 \\ -\ 25 \\ \hline 13 \\ -\ 10 \\ \hline 35 \\ -\ 35 \\ \hline 0 \end{array}$$

7. D
$$\begin{array}{r} 4 \\ 12\overline{)48} \\ -\ 48 \\ \hline 0 \end{array}$$

8. H
$$\begin{array}{r} 72 \\ 6\overline{)432} \\ -\ 42 \\ \hline 12 \\ -\ 12 \\ \hline 0 \end{array}$$

9. E
$$\begin{array}{r} 4{,}160 \\ 2\overline{)8{,}320} \\ -\ 8 \\ \hline 03 \\ -\ 2 \\ \hline 12 \\ -\ 12 \\ \hline 00 \end{array}$$

10. F
$$\begin{array}{r} 7 \\ 6\overline{)42} \\ -\ 42 \\ \hline 0 \end{array}$$

Lesson 8 Practice (page 29)

1. C
$$\begin{array}{r} 1\ \text{R}3 \\ 6\overline{)9} \\ -\ 6 \\ \hline 3 \end{array}$$

2. K
$$\begin{array}{r} 1\ \text{R}1 \\ 6\overline{)7} \\ -\ 6 \\ \hline 1 \end{array}$$

3. A
$$\begin{array}{r} 2\ \text{R}1 \\ 2\overline{)5} \\ -\ 4 \\ \hline 1 \end{array}$$

4. G
$$\begin{array}{r} 2 \text{ R1} \\ 7)\overline{15} \\ -14 \\ \hline 1 \end{array}$$

5. C
$$\begin{array}{r} 2 \text{ R2} \\ 3)\overline{8} \\ -6 \\ \hline 2 \end{array}$$

6. F
$$\begin{array}{r} 1 \text{ R1} \\ 8)\overline{9} \\ -8 \\ \hline 1 \end{array}$$

7. B
$$\begin{array}{r} 156 \text{ R4} \\ 6)\overline{940} \\ -6 \\ \hline 34 \\ -30 \\ \hline 40 \\ -36 \\ \hline 4 \end{array}$$

8. G
$$\begin{array}{r} 3 \text{ R1} \\ 2)\overline{7} \\ -6 \\ \hline 1 \end{array}$$

9. C
$$\begin{array}{r} 1 \text{ R2} \\ 6)\overline{8} \\ -6 \\ \hline 2 \end{array}$$

10. K
$$\begin{array}{r} 2 \text{ R6} \\ 40)\overline{86} \\ -80 \\ \hline 6 \end{array}$$

TABE Review: Division of Whole Numbers (pages 30–31)

1. B
$$\begin{array}{r} 2,600 \\ 3)\overline{7,800} \\ -6 \\ \hline 18 \\ -18 \\ \hline 000 \end{array}$$ [Division of Whole Numbers—No Remainder]

2. G
$$\begin{array}{r} 1 \text{ R2} \\ 5)\overline{7} \\ -5 \\ \hline 2 \end{array}$$ [Division of Whole Numbers—Remainder]

3. D
$$\begin{array}{r} 94 \\ 8)\overline{752} \\ -72 \\ \hline 32 \\ -32 \\ \hline 0 \end{array}$$ [Division of Whole Numbers—No Remainder]

4. H
$$\begin{array}{r} 4 \\ 20)\overline{80} \\ -80 \\ \hline 0 \end{array}$$ [Division of Whole Numbers—No Remainder]

5. A
$$\begin{array}{r} 1 \text{ R1} \\ 7)\overline{8} \\ -7 \\ \hline 1 \end{array}$$ [Division of Whole Numbers—Remainder]

6. H
$$\begin{array}{r} 7 \\ 11)\overline{77} \\ -77 \\ \hline 0 \end{array}$$ [Division of Whole Numbers—No Remainder]

7. E
$$\begin{array}{r} 1 \text{ R2} \\ 7)\overline{9} \\ -7 \\ \hline 2 \end{array}$$ [Division of Whole Numbers—Remainder]

8. G
$$\begin{array}{r} 1 \text{ R4} \\ 5)\overline{9} \\ -5 \\ \hline 4 \end{array}$$ [Division of Whole Numbers—Remainder]

9. A
$$\begin{array}{r} 4,652 \\ 2)\overline{9,304} \\ -8 \\ \hline 13 \\ -12 \\ \hline 10 \\ -10 \\ \hline 04 \\ -4 \\ \hline 0 \end{array}$$ [Division of Whole Numbers—No Remainder]

10. G
$$\begin{array}{r} 1 \text{ R3} \\ 5)\overline{8} \\ -5 \\ \hline 3 \end{array}$$ [Division of Whole Numbers—Remainder]

11. E
$$\begin{array}{r} 9 \\ 3)\overline{27} \\ -27 \\ \hline 0 \end{array}$$ [Division of Whole Numbers—No Remainder]

12. G
$$\begin{array}{r} 8 \\ 8)\overline{64} \\ -64 \\ \hline 0 \end{array}$$ [Division of Whole Numbers—No Remainder]

13. C
$$\begin{array}{r} 8 \\ 10)\overline{80} \\ -80 \\ \hline 0 \end{array}$$ [Division of Whole Numbers—No Remainder]

14. H
$$\begin{array}{r} 2 \text{ R1} \\ 3)\overline{7} \\ -6 \\ \hline 1 \end{array}$$ [Division of Whole Numbers—Remainder]

15. A
$$\begin{array}{r} 2,884 \\ 3)\overline{8,652} \\ -6 \\ \hline 26 \\ -24 \\ \hline 25 \\ -24 \\ \hline 12 \\ -12 \\ \hline 0 \end{array}$$ [Division of Whole Numbers—No Remainder]

16. K
$$\begin{array}{r} 1 \text{ R2} \\ 3)\overline{5} \\ -3 \\ \hline 2 \end{array}$$ [Division of Whole Numbers—Remainder]

17. C
$$\begin{array}{r} 1,230 \\ 7)\overline{8,610} \\ -7 \\ \hline 16 \\ -14 \\ \hline 21 \\ -21 \\ \hline 00 \end{array}$$ [Division of Whole Numbers—No Remainder]

18. K
$$\begin{array}{r} 33 \\ 9)\overline{297} \\ -27 \\ \hline 27 \\ -27 \\ \hline 0 \end{array}$$ [Division of Whole Numbers—No Remainder]

Lesson 9 Practice (page 33)

1. C
$$\begin{array}{r} 73.0 \\ +\ 2.4 \\ \hline 75.4 \end{array}$$

2. J
$$\begin{array}{r} 12.0 \\ +\ 4.2 \\ \hline 16.2 \end{array}$$

3. A
$$\begin{array}{r} 25.0 \\ +\ 4.1 \\ \hline 29.1 \end{array}$$

4. K
$$
\begin{array}{r}
4.5 \\
+\ 3.4 \\
\hline
7.9
\end{array}
$$

5. C
$$
\begin{array}{r}
34.0 \\
+\ 3.1 \\
\hline
37.1
\end{array}
$$

6. G
$$
\begin{array}{r}
4.2 \\
+\ 3.0 \\
\hline
7.2
\end{array}
$$

7. A
$$
\begin{array}{r}
62.0 \\
+\ 3.7 \\
\hline
65.7
\end{array}
$$

8. H
$$
\begin{array}{r}
2.0 \\
+\ 4.7 \\
\hline
6.7
\end{array}
$$

9. E
$$
\begin{array}{r}
42.0 \\
+\ 6.9 \\
\hline
48.9
\end{array}
$$

10. J
$$
\begin{array}{r}
5.3 \\
+\ 3.0 \\
\hline
8.3
\end{array}
$$

Lesson 10 Practice (page 35)

1. A
$$
\begin{array}{r}
{}^{1}\overset{13}{\cancel{5}}2.\overset{3}{\cancel{4}}\overset{10}{0} \\
-\ 0.76 \\
\hline
51.64
\end{array}
$$

2. H
$$
\begin{array}{r}
\overset{5}{3}\overset{9}{6}.\overset{9}{0}\overset{10}{0}0 \\
-\ 3.526 \\
\hline
32.474
\end{array}
$$

3. D
$$
\begin{array}{r}
{}^{2}\overset{13}{\cancel{1}}3.\overset{3}{\cancel{4}}\overset{10}{0} \\
-\ 0.56 \\
\hline
12.84
\end{array}
$$

4. K
$$
\begin{array}{r}
\overset{7}{1}\overset{9}{8}.\overset{9}{0}\overset{10}{0}0 \\
-\ 5.719 \\
\hline
12.281
\end{array}
$$

5. C
$$
\begin{array}{r}
{}^{4}\overset{12}{1}5.\overset{2}{\cancel{3}}\overset{10}{0} \\
-\ .73 \\
\hline
14.57
\end{array}
$$

---

6. F
$$
\begin{array}{r}
{}^{813}\overset{3\ 9}{9}4.\overset{9}{0}\overset{10}{0}0 \\
-\ 6.759 \\
\hline
87.241
\end{array}
$$

7. B
$$
\begin{array}{r}
{}^{6\ 18}\overset{8}{5}\overset{10}{7}.\overset{}{9}0 \\
-\ 0.93 \\
\hline
56.97
\end{array}
$$

8. K
$$
\begin{array}{r}
{}^{711}\overset{1\ 9}{8}2.\overset{9}{0}\overset{10}{0}0 \\
-\ 4.672 \\
\hline
77.328
\end{array}
$$

9. C
$$
\begin{array}{r}
{}^{11}\overset{3}{4}4.\overset{1}{2}\overset{10}{0} \\
-\ 0.81 \\
\hline
43.39
\end{array}
$$

10. G
$$
\begin{array}{r}
\overset{4}{7}5.\overset{9}{0}\overset{10}{0} \\
-\ 3.72 \\
\hline
71.28
\end{array}
$$

Lesson 11 Practice (page 37)

1. A
$$
\begin{array}{r}
0.7 \\
\times\ 3 \\
\hline
2.1
\end{array}
$$

2. F
$$
\begin{array}{r}
{}^{21}0.752 \\
\times\ 500 \\
\hline
376.000
\end{array}
$$

3. B
$$
\begin{array}{r}
{}^{534}784.6 \\
\times\ 0.7 \\
\hline
549.22
\end{array}
$$

4. H
$$
\begin{array}{r}
6 \\
\times\ 0.6 \\
\hline
3.6
\end{array}
$$

5. E
$$
\begin{array}{r}
{}^{7}3.8 \\
\times\ 1.9 \\
\hline
{}^{1}342 \\
+\ 380 \\
\hline
7.22
\end{array}
$$

6. K
$$
\begin{array}{r}
{}^{51}562.1 \\
\times\ 0.9 \\
\hline
505.89
\end{array}
$$

7. C
$$
\begin{array}{r}
{}^{1\ 22}0.469 \\
\times\ 300 \\
\hline
140.700
\end{array}
$$

---

8. J
$$
\begin{array}{r}
0.4 \\
\times\ 7 \\
\hline
2.8
\end{array}
$$

9. A
$$
\begin{array}{r}
{}^{5}\ {}^{2}6.7 \\
\times\ 8.4 \\
\hline
{}^{1}268 \\
+\ 5360 \\
\hline
56.28
\end{array}
$$

10. G
$$
\begin{array}{r}
8 \\
\times\ 0.6 \\
\hline
4.8
\end{array}
$$

TABE Review: Decimals (pages 38–39)

1. E
$$
\begin{array}{r}
\overset{510}{14.6}0 \\
-\ 0.35 \\
\hline
14.25
\end{array}
$$
[Subtraction of Decimals]

2. H
$$
\begin{array}{r}
{}^{2\ 2}351.7 \\
\times\ 0.4 \\
\hline
140.68
\end{array}
$$
[Multiplication of Decimals]

3. A
$$
\begin{array}{r}
21.0 \\
+\ 2.3 \\
\hline
23.3
\end{array}
$$
[Addition of Decimals]

4. G
$$
\begin{array}{r}
\overset{510}{37.6}0 \\
-\ 0.34 \\
\hline
37.26
\end{array}
$$
[Subtraction of Decimals]

5. A
$$
\begin{array}{r}
7 \\
\times\ 0.9 \\
\hline
6.3
\end{array}
$$
[Multiplication of Decimals]

6. J
$$
\begin{array}{r}
81.0 \\
+\ 1.6 \\
\hline
82.6
\end{array}
$$
[Addition of Decimals]

7. C
$$
\begin{array}{r}
{}^{1\ 12}\overset{2}{7}2.3\overset{10}{\cancel{0}} \\
-\ 0.41 \\
\hline
71.89
\end{array}
$$
[Subtraction of Decimals]

8. K $\overset{\scriptstyle 1\ 5}{}$ 0.819 [Multiplication of
$\times\ \ 600$ Decimals]
491.400

9. C $\overset{\scriptstyle 2\ 9\ 9\ 10}{53.000}$ [Subtraction of
$-\ \ \ 1.245$ Decimals]
51.755

10. G 6.4 [Addition of
$+\ 2.0$ Decimals]
8.4

11. D 0.5 [Multiplication of
$\times\ \ \ 9$ Decimals]
4.5

12. H 13.0 [Addition of
$+\ \ .67$ Decimals]
13.67

13. D $\overset{\scriptstyle 4\ 9\ 9\ 10}{45.000}$ [Subtraction of
$-\ \ 2.741$ Decimals]
42.259

14. K 6.0 [Addition of
$+\ 3.1$ Decimals]
9.1

15. A $\overset{\scriptstyle 4\ 10}{23.5\cancel{0}}$ [Subtraction of
$-\ \ .34$ Decimals]
23.16

16. J $\overset{\scriptstyle 1}{\overset{\scriptstyle 1}{}}$ 9.2 [Multiplication of
$\times\ 7.5$ Decimals]
$\overset{\scriptstyle 1}{}$
460
$+\ 6,440$
69.00

17. B 51.0 [Addition of
$+\ \ 8.4$ Decimals]
59.4

18. G 5 [Multiplication
$\times\ 0.8$ of Decimals]
4.0

Lesson 12 Practice (page 41)

1. D

$$\frac{3}{5} = \frac{3}{5} + \frac{1}{5} = \frac{4}{5}$$
$$+\frac{1}{5}$$

2. G

$$\frac{3}{4} = \frac{3}{4} + \frac{3}{4} = \frac{6}{4} = 1\frac{2}{4} = 1\frac{1}{2}$$
$$+\frac{3}{4}$$

3. A

$$\frac{5}{6} = \frac{5}{6} + \frac{4}{6} = \frac{9}{6} = 1\frac{3}{6} = 1\frac{1}{2}$$
$$+\frac{4}{6}$$

4. F

$$\frac{3}{9} = \frac{3}{9} + \frac{4}{9} = \frac{7}{9}$$
$$+\frac{4}{9}$$

5. C

$$\frac{5}{8} = \frac{5}{8} + \frac{7}{8} = \frac{12}{8} = 1\frac{4}{8} = 1\frac{1}{2}$$
$$+\frac{7}{8}$$

6. K

$$\frac{5}{9} = \frac{5}{9} + \frac{1}{9} = \frac{6}{9} = \frac{2}{3}$$
$$+\frac{1}{9}$$

7. D

$$\frac{2}{4} = \frac{2}{4} + \frac{1}{4} = \frac{3}{4}$$
$$+\frac{1}{4}$$

8. G

$$\frac{2}{5} = \frac{2}{5} + \frac{3}{5} = \frac{5}{5} = 1$$
$$+\frac{3}{5}$$

---

9. C

$$\frac{3}{6} = \frac{3}{6} + \frac{1}{6} = \frac{4}{6} = \frac{2}{3}$$
$$+\frac{1}{6}$$

10. K

$$\frac{8}{9} = \frac{8}{9} + \frac{5}{9} = \frac{13}{9} = 1\frac{4}{9}$$
$$+\frac{5}{9}$$

Lesson 13 Practice (page 43)

1. C

$$\frac{15}{21} = \frac{15}{21} - \frac{12}{21} = \frac{3}{21} = \frac{1}{7}$$
$$-\frac{12}{21}$$

2. J

$$\frac{5}{6} - \frac{1}{6} = \frac{4}{6} = \frac{2}{3}$$

3. E

$$\frac{6}{8} - \frac{4}{8} = \frac{2}{8} = \frac{1}{4}$$

4. G

$$\frac{19}{34} = \frac{19}{34} - \frac{11}{34} = \frac{8}{34} = \frac{4}{17}$$
$$-\frac{11}{34}$$

5. D

$$\frac{6}{7} - \frac{5}{7} = \frac{1}{7}$$

6. K

$$\frac{26}{27} = \frac{26}{27} - \frac{8}{27} = \frac{18}{27} = \frac{2}{3}$$
$$-\frac{8}{27}$$

7. C

$$\frac{8}{11} - \frac{2}{11} = \frac{6}{11}$$

---

8. J

$$\frac{21}{30} = \frac{21}{30} - \frac{6}{30} = \frac{15}{30} = \frac{1}{2}$$
$$-\frac{6}{30}$$

9. B

$$\frac{4}{5} - \frac{4}{5} = 0$$

10. G

$$\frac{12}{18} = \frac{12}{18} - \frac{8}{18} = \frac{4}{18} = \frac{2}{9}$$
$$-\frac{8}{18}$$

TABE Review: Fractions (pages 44–45)

1. D

$$\frac{7}{15} = \frac{7}{15} - \frac{3}{15} = \frac{4}{15}$$
$$-\frac{3}{15}$$

[Subtraction of Fractions]

2. G

$$\frac{7}{12} + \frac{3}{12} = \frac{10}{12} = \frac{5}{6}$$

[Addition of Fractions]

3. B

$$\frac{5}{7} = \frac{5}{7} + \frac{1}{7} = \frac{6}{7}$$
$$+\frac{1}{7}$$

[Addition of Fractions]

4. J

$$\frac{10}{15} - \frac{7}{15} = \frac{3}{15} = \frac{1}{5}$$

[Subtraction or Fractions]

5. B

$$\frac{3}{6} = \frac{3}{6} + \frac{4}{6} = \frac{7}{6} = 1\frac{1}{6}$$
$$+\frac{4}{6}$$

[Addition of Fractions]

6. H

$$\frac{6}{8} - \frac{3}{8} = \frac{3}{8}$$

[Subtraction of Fractions]

7. A

$$\frac{7}{9} - \frac{1}{9} = \frac{6}{9} = \frac{2}{3}$$

[Subtraction of Fractions]

8. H

$$\frac{2}{4} = \frac{2}{4} + \frac{3}{4} = \frac{5}{4} = 1\frac{1}{4}$$
$$+\frac{3}{4}$$

[Addition of Fractions]

9. B

$$\frac{8}{9} - \frac{5}{9} = \frac{3}{9} = \frac{1}{3}$$

[Subtraction of Fractions]

10. G

$$\frac{7}{9} = \frac{7}{9} + \frac{8}{9} = \frac{15}{9} = 1\frac{6}{9} = 1\frac{2}{3}$$
$$+\frac{8}{9}$$

[Addition of Fractions]

11. E

$$\frac{7}{10} = \frac{7}{10} - \frac{3}{10} = \frac{4}{10} = \frac{2}{5}$$
$$-\frac{3}{10}$$

[Subtraction of Fractions]

12. H

$$\frac{20}{24} = \frac{20}{24} - \frac{8}{24} = \frac{12}{24} = \frac{1}{2}$$
$$-\frac{8}{24}$$

[Subtraction of Fractions]

13. A

$$\frac{3}{7} = \frac{3}{7} + \frac{2}{7} = \frac{5}{7}$$
$$+\frac{2}{7}$$

[Addition of Fractions]

14. J

$$\frac{6}{20} + \frac{5}{20} + \frac{4}{20} = \frac{15}{20} = \frac{3}{4}$$

[Addition of Fractions]

15. B

$$\frac{4}{8} = \frac{4}{8} + \frac{1}{8} = \frac{5}{8}$$
$$+\frac{1}{8}$$

[Addition of Fractions]

16. F

$$\frac{10}{11} = \frac{10}{11} - \frac{9}{11} = \frac{1}{11}$$
$$-\frac{9}{11}$$

[Subtraction of Fractions]

Performance Assessment Sample A (page 46)

A. A

$$\begin{array}{r} {}^{1\;13}2\cancel{3}\cancel{9} \\ -\;42 \\ \hline 197 \end{array}$$

1. B
$$\begin{array}{r} 654 \\ +\ 43 \\ \hline 697 \end{array}$$
[Addition of Whole Numbers— No Regrouping]

2. G
$$13\overline{)39}\ \ \ ^{3}$$
$$\begin{array}{r} -\ 39 \\ \hline 0 \end{array}$$
[Division of Whole Numbers—No Remainder]

3. C
$$\begin{array}{r} 61 \\ \times\ 13 \\ \hline 183 \\ +\ 610 \\ \hline 793 \end{array}$$
[Multiplication of Whole Numbers— No Regrouping]

4. F
$$\begin{array}{r} ^{2}\ \\ 8 \\ 7 \\ +\ 6 \\ \hline 21 \end{array}$$
[Addition of Whole Numbers— With Regrouping]

5. B
$$6\overline{)36}\ \ ^{6}$$
$$\begin{array}{r} -\ 36 \\ \hline 0 \end{array}$$
[Division of Whole Numbers—No Remainder]

6. K
$$\begin{array}{r} ^{4\ 17} \\ 35\!\!\not{7} \\ -\ 29 \\ \hline 328 \end{array}$$
[Subtraction of Whole Numbers— Regrouping]

7. B
$$\begin{array}{r} 813 \\ \times\ 64 \\ \hline ^{11\ 1} \\ 3,252 \\ +\ 48,780 \\ \hline 52,032 \end{array}$$
[Multiplication of Whole Numbers— Regrouping]

8. H
$$\begin{array}{r} ^{7\ 12} \\ 2,8\!\!\not{2}4 \\ -\ 734 \\ \hline 2,090 \end{array}$$
[Subtraction of Whole Numbers— Regrouping]

9. E
$$\begin{array}{r} ^{5\ \not{3}\ 11} \\ 1,6\!\!\not{4}\!\!\not{1} \\ -\ 568 \\ \hline 1,073 \end{array}$$
[Subtraction of Whole Numbers— Regrouping]

10. G
$$\begin{array}{r} 589 \\ -\ 244 \\ \hline 345 \end{array}$$
[Subtraction of Whole Numbers— No Regrouping]

11. C
$$\begin{array}{r} 210 \\ \times\ 5 \\ \hline 1,050 \end{array}$$
[Multiplication of Whole Numbers— No Regrouping]

12. H
$$\begin{array}{r} ^{1} \\ 2.3 \\ \times\ 5.1 \\ \hline 2\ 3 \\ +\ 11\ 5\ 0 \\ \hline 11.7\ 3 \end{array}$$
[Multiplication of Decimals]

13. B
$$\begin{array}{r} ^{3\ 2} \\ 0.6\ 5\ 3 \\ \times\ 700 \\ \hline 457.100 \end{array}$$
[Multiplication of Decimals]

14. J
$$\begin{array}{r} ^{6\ 10} \\ 27.\!\!\not{1}\!\!\not{0} \\ -\ 0.47 \\ \hline 26.63 \end{array}$$
[Subtraction of Decimals]

15. A
$$\frac{2}{5} = \frac{2}{5} + \frac{1}{5} = \frac{3}{5}$$
$$+\ \frac{1}{5}$$
[Addition of Fractions]

16. K
$$\begin{array}{r} ^{1} \\ 356 \\ +\ 527 \\ \hline 883 \end{array}$$
[Addition of Whole Numbers— Regrouping]

17. C
$$5\overline{)7}\ \ ^{1\ R2}$$
$$\begin{array}{r} -\ 5 \\ \hline 2 \end{array}$$
[Division of Whole Numbers— Remainder]

18. J
$$\frac{11}{12} - \frac{3}{12} = \frac{8}{12} = \frac{2}{3}$$
[Subtraction of Fractions]

19. B
$$6\overline{)3,702}\ \ ^{617}$$
$$\begin{array}{r} -\ 36 \\ \hline 10 \\ -\ 6 \\ \hline 42 \\ -\ 42 \\ \hline 0 \end{array}$$
[Division of Whole Numbers—No Remainder]

20. J
$$\begin{array}{r} ^{1} \\ 9,423 \\ +\ 7 \\ \hline 9,430 \end{array}$$
[Addition of Whole Numbers— Regrouping]

21. A
$$\begin{array}{r} ^{2\ 9\ 9\ 10} \\ 63.\!\!\not{0}\!\!\not{0}\!\!\not{0} \\ -\ 1.756 \\ \hline 61.244 \end{array}$$
[Subtraction of Decimals]

22. K
$$\begin{array}{r} 21 \\ \times\ 0 \\ \hline 0 \end{array}$$
[Multiplication of Whole Numbers—No Regrouping]

23. E
$$\frac{7}{8} = \frac{7}{8} + \frac{3}{8} = \frac{10}{8} = 1\ \frac{2}{8} = 1\ \frac{1}{4}$$
$$+\ \frac{3}{8}$$
[Addition of Fractions]

24. F
$$\begin{array}{r} ^{1} \\ 62 \\ \times\ 35 \\ \hline ^{1} \\ 310 \\ +\ 1,860 \\ \hline 2,170 \end{array}$$
[Multiplication of Whole Numbers— Regrouping]

25. A
$$\frac{9}{14} = \frac{9}{14} - \frac{5}{14} = \frac{4}{14} = \frac{2}{7}$$
$$-\ \frac{5}{14}$$
[Subtraction of Fractions]